A SONG FROM THE ASHES

No life is exempt from resurrection.
Even a seemingly wasted life
carries the seed for redemption.

Printed in the United States of America
ISBN: 978-1-63385-102-3
Library of Congress Number: 9781633851023

Design and Printing:
Word Association Publishers
205 Fifth Avenue
Tarentum, Pennsylvania 15084
www.wordassociation.com

A SONG FROM THE ASHES

No life is exempt from resurrection.
Even a seemingly wasted life
carries the seed for redemption.

MEMOIRS BY MICHELINE BARKLEY

PREFACE

Only be careful and watch yourselves closely so that you do not forget the things your eyes have seen or let them slip from your heart as long as you live. Teach them to your children and to their children after them.
—Deuteronomy 4:9 NIV

Before the Israelites crossed the Jordan River to the long-awaited Promised Land, God instructed them to tell the stories of their sufferings and joys to their children so the following generations would know and remember it was God who had set them free. I've learned a great deal from this story; so it is with me. I want my children to remember my sufferings and joys in their walks with Christ.

I want my children to know where I came from, so to speak. My hope is that in knowing what I experienced, they will learn from me and understand why I am the way I am—the way God formed and shaped me through my experiences.

This is of special importance to me because I grew up without having much of a relationship with my parents. My father wasn't around, and because my mother worked and went to school at night to improve our lives, I had a great sense of emptiness in my life as a child.. I didn't know my own history as a child—I had no stories, photos—nothing.

When we left Vietnam, we left our extended family and the only home my mother had ever known. We started over with almost nothing. I have few mementos from my early childhood and some mere scraps of memories and stories, but I will share them here so my children will be able to understand that part of their heritage.

Ultimately, I hope all readers will see that God's plan is perfect. Even when our lives seem to be a mess and out of control, there's a purpose for every experience, good and bad. When we choose to have a thoughtful, sincere relationship with God, he reveals his purpose for our lives. Knowing our true purpose for life and cultivating that relationship with God will prevent us from wandering aimlessly and will help us live fully and purposefully for him. Only then can we discover true joy.

I've shared my story in brief forms many times since I was about thirteen. The fact that so many people have expressed interest in it made me realize that what seemed an ordinary life to me was much more than that to others. When I was a young teenager, where I was born would come up simply as a matter of conversation. But when people learned I had come to America from Vietnam, their questions quickly followed.

Of course, I loved that my friends were interested, so I started sharing bits and pieces of my story, although only with few close friends at first. My teenage discussions often turned into a type of contest about whose life was worse; some of my closest friends had alcoholic, bipolar, or divorced parents among other problems.

When I got older, though, many people encouraged me, pointing out that I was a survivor and had needed to be strong to handle everything that had come my way. Maybe they hadn't run into many people who had such crazy circumstances in their lives and they were intrigued and sometimes amazed and in awe of my story.

Sadly, that encouragement led for a time to a kind of self-aggrandizement: "Yeah, I did that." After coming back to God later in my life, I realized it was in fact all God's strength—none of my own. All I had experienced was him shaping me for his purpose; that realization hit me like a ton of bricks. It was similar to reading the "Footprints" poem for the first time. My pride drove my anger as I read, "I noticed that during the low periods of my life, when I was suffering from anguish, sorrow, or defeat, I could see only one set of footprints." *Yeah, why did I suffer alone?* I thought. "Why, when I needed you most, have you not been there for me?" *Yes, yes, yes—why did you abandon me?* "The years when you have seen only one set of footprints, my child, are when I carried you." *Oh wow!*

But I still couldn't understand why I had survived what I had survived. Why had bad things happened to me in the first place? What was the point, the meaning of all my struggles? It was just my life; I knew nothing else with which to compare it. At last, I'm seeing God's plan for my life, knowing my purpose and how God wants me to accomplish it, and now I know he has been preparing me all along.

My desire is to touch the hearts and lives of others who have struggled through adversity to give them hope that their suffering is not in vain.

Each time I tell my story, I exhale. Now, finally, all my wounds have healed. The scars left behind don't bother me or interfere with my life; they're just reminders. I'll always wear them in the form of my personality and character, but I believe that's a good thing; I like who I am. Not everyone else will, but that's okay, because there's only one person's opinion and love that matters to me, my Lord and Savior's.

CHAPTER ONE
A FEW "REMEMORIES"

Remember the days of old,
Consider the generations long past.
Ask your father, and he will tell you,
your elders, and they will explain to you.
—Deuteronomy 32:7 NIV

My daughter, Michaela, would often tell me, "You don't have a good rememory," which is true. Many gaps break up my memories, and though I can now see how God used events early in my life to shape the person I was to become, many details of my childhood have faded. Still, I do have some memories of my early life and a few stories I've gathered over the years, and I know that it's important to remember—but not to live in—those "olden" days as I move forward.

All children seem to love to hear the story of their births, and I was no different. Mine, however, was tinged with threats of danger and sadness. At the time of my birth in Vietnam in 1969, my father, James, a U.S. soldier, was on temporary duty in Cam Ranh Bay, about 180 miles from my mother's home. He received a call, according to the story I was told, on the evening of March 17 that my mother, Mot, had gone into labor. He immediately flew by helicopter to Da Nang and on to our hometown, Tan Son Nhat, where he took a taxi to the Seventh Day Adventist hospital in Phu Nhuan. He arrived shortly after midnight on March 18 and walked up a ramp into the maternity ward. Looking to his left, into the birthing room, he was just in the nick of time to see my head crowning.

Mom was in good spirits; she talked with Dad after the birth when my father mentioned to the nursing staff that she had a history of hemorrhaging after delivery. Just as he was warning them, she began to bleed severely, but the doctors quickly controlled that. My dad said Mom was extremely pale from the loss of blood, but by the next day, she had thankfully recovered, and both of us were sent home in good health. We were very lucky that my father had made it to the hospital in time and had thought to warn the doctors.

My mother chose my name; she told me it was a derivative of the name of a French queen. I'm not certain that's true; I've never done much research into it, but I like to think it is. The next day, my father went to the courthouse to record my birth, Since apparently nothing was done quickly there without a little "greasing of the palms," Dad slipped some money to the person handling the records, and he issued my Vietnamese birth certificate.

There was one small, comical mishap though. My dad, being something of a clueless male, spelled my name Michelene. My mother had to make another trip to the courthouse to have it corrected to Micheline. My father had originally wanted to name me Belinda, but my mother had objected. My name was a source of pain in my childhood. Children teased me mercilessly by calling me everything from "Michelin Tires" to "Mitsubishi."

The sadness associated with my birth was the unexpected death of my paternal grandmother. When I was only ten days old, my father had to fly home to the United States to bury his mother. My grandmother had been killed by a car as she crossed a street in Yuba City, California. My father has indicated that she suffered from depression; he felt she had thrown herself in front of that car. She'd had her share of life's problems.

I can still picture my childhood home. Tan Son Hoa was a small town in the current Ho Chi Minh Province. It has a very small population now, but it's only a few miles from Ho

Chi Minh City, formerly Saigon. In the early 1970s, I would go to a fish market there with our nanny Chi Sau.

I was only two or three when, on a visit to the fish market, I became separated from her and began to cry a flood of tears. I remember being incredibly scared because I had lost her and because all I could see around me were fish heads all over the ground. I was terrified. I sobbed until a stranger picked me up. He stood me on top of one of the makeshift tables (really just plywood on boxes) and yelled to draw everyone's attention. I have the impression he was calling out that there was a little lost girl, and heads started to turn to me. Soon enough, Chi Sau came out of the crowd. I was so happy to see her!

Our home life was unconventional by most standards today; at one point, my parents ran a brothel out of the main floor of our home, where we lived on the top floor. Yet some of the pieces of the memories I have of my early years are still pleasant. I had five older siblings, ranging from two to eleven years older than me.

One of the rooms of our home was painted a lime green, and the dining room chairs were made of dark wood and had tall, carved backs. I recall that we had a dog that once had puppies. I remember gleefully discovering her in a closet shortly after she had given birth to a litter of adorable, fluffy puppies.

At another time, I recall hiding under a table in our home in fear of something, but I'm not sure of what. I know, however, that I did that often. Living in a war zone with parents who were often at odds with each other, I'm sure I may have had many reasons for that behavior.

My mother and father had a violent relationship. They loved each other, but they drank and they battled emotional problems such as jealousy that led to frequent arguments. I recall my sister saying that weapons were used in some of their fights. That fits with my impressions of their relationship.

When I was two, my father left us with only the clothes on his back and his wallet—that's it. If he had packed or if my mom had known that he was leaving, he told me later, he feared she might have killed him.

By 1975, my father was a fading memory. He had returned to his home in the United States, and my mother was left to care for her children on her own. Mom hadn't even considered immigrating to America earlier. She'd heard that Americans were very prejudiced, and she feared we would be mistreated as foreigners. It soon became apparent, however, that she didn't have any other choice. She had mixed

(Vietnamese-American) children, and the Communists hated Americans. As the North Vietnamese troops progressed
toward Saigon with the goal of reuniting the county under
Communist rule, she rightly feared for our lives.

As the years have passed, documentaries and arti-
cles have reinforced the fear my mother felt. After the war,
other children taunted and pummeled the mixed kids. They
mocked the way they looked—so much like the American
enemy. Everyone looked down on mixed children; they assumed their mothers were prostitutes (and in some cases
that was true) even though many of them were products of
longer-term relationships, including marriage, as I had been.
Their destiny was to become beggars, living on the streets.
They were referred to as "children of the dust," insignificant
and lowly as dirt. Neighbors would call them "half-breed
dogs." Rumors of their massacres and threats of being set
on fire spread but didn't come to fruition; nonetheless, the
Communists weren't kind. Many orphanages were closed,
and many of these children were sent off to rural work farms
and reeducation camps. They were denied education, government assistance, and societal acceptance. Many contem-
plated suicide; some followed through.

With no education or skills, the children of the dust became vulnerable to drugs, gangs, and prison. Had we stayed in Vietnam, I would have lived under a dark cloud all my life. Even though I am an American citizen, I feel it's not a right but a privileged to live in America, I count myself immensely blessed.

At one point, my mother was so desperate to get her children out of Vietnam that she went to an American orphanage and tried to have all six of us adopted in America. When she was told we couldn't all be placed together, she couldn't go through with it.

And so, amid mounting chaos, my mother packed one suitcase for herself and her six children and began the journey to the United States. When we left Vietnam, I was six; my next oldest brother, James, or Jimmy, was eight; Maurice (Moe) was eleven; Ninh (Phoung) was fourteen; Nguyet (Letty) was fifteen; and Canh, the eldest, was seventeen.

My mother had to bribe someone so Canh could come with us. Males of draft age were to stay and fight, and since he was a child of my mother's first marriage, he didn't have American citizenship. My mother gave a driver money not to expose my brother. God worked through this situation to keep my family together all the way to America.

I don't know how long it took her to complete the paperwork, but I remember seeing photocopies of some documents, including applications for passports, when I was older. In particular, I remember my black-and-white passport photograph; I was so sad, and traces of my tears are visible in the picture. I remember not wanting to have my picture taken. These papers also had my father's name and information about the man who was such a mystery to me—where and when he was born, his parents' names, and so on. I spent many years imagining all that I didn't know about my father.

So many of the bits of memory that I have from that time are difficult, but I'm reminded that throughout the Bible, God used people from a variety of backgrounds to accomplish his work. One of the most obvious is Moses, but there were many—Samuel, Deborah, Ruth, Matthew, and the rest of those simple fishermen and hated tax collectors whom Jesus had called to follow him.

When we're open to God's will, he will use us, and at the same time, we are told to remember from where it is we have come. I believe that remembering my past has given me a heart to serve others, and I hope my story will encourage others to do the same.

CHAPTER TWO
TURNING POINT

Sometimes the course of our lives depends on what we
do or don't do in a few seconds, a heartbeat, when we
either seize the opportunity, or just miss it.
Miss the moment and you never get a chance again.
—Aidan Chambers, *Dying to Know You*

My husband, Matthew, and I disagree about the biggest turning point in my life. I think it was the day I met him, but he thinks it must have been when I came to America, so I'll share both stories. (My story about Matt is in chapter 10.)

Moving to a new country would be a big change in anyone's life, and for me, it was truly a change for the better. Because I arrived in America at such a young age, the details are fuzzy, but I'll do my best to relate them. (As a side note, I do find it interesting the things we remember and the things we forget.)

My family and I left Vietnam just three days before the fall of Saigon on April 30, 1975, in the midst of the maddening wave of desperation that swept through the city. The South Vietnamese were exhausted by years of war, and they were frightened by what would become of their lives if they didn't get out before the Communists took over.

In the final eighteen hours before the city surrendered, 7,000 Vietnamese and American citizens were moved out of Saigon in the largest helicopter evacuation in history—Operation Frequent Wind. In the weeks prior, however, a steady and increasingly desperate flood of people left; they totaled in the tens of thousands. One estimate is that Operation New Life, which processed South Vietnamese refugees through Guam and on to settlement in the United States, assisted 110,000 civilians in the final weeks of the war.

On the day we left, we took a taxi from our house to the American embassy. Our one suitcase sat on my lap during the ride. I vividly remember that little tan suitcase that held all we possessed in the world. Back then, they were hard cases, not like the canvas or leather pieces of luggage we have today. The only clothing I had packed was a traditional Vietnamese dress called an *áo dài* ("ow yi," pronounced like *hi*). It was a long, fitted tunic with slits up both sides to the waist; loose, flowing white pants were worn underneath. Mine was bright yellow and made of a thin material because of the warm climate. I had matching clogs. The bases and soles of the shoes were wood, and the top part was yellow leather decorated with a pattern of holes all over. I loved those shoes.

From the American embassy, we rode a bus to Tan Son Nhut Airbase. After the bus ride, the next thing I remember was a herd of civilians, my family included, walking toward a giant airplane. It was as big as a whale and shaped like one too. I later learned it was a C-5 cargo plane used to transport large volumes of just about anything—in our case, people. The airplane's belly was open. The gate was down. We walked up a ramp to enter the plane. My six-year-old self felt so small next to this behemoth. The ceiling of the plane was high, and it was dark inside.

I remember a row of fold-down seats attached to the sides of plane; they had a webbing of fabric woven in two directions, just like some lawn chairs, but these weren't brightly colored—just dark green. I had no idea then what they were, but I now realize they were normally used as seats for crew and passengers. We, however, didn't sit on these seats, and in retrospect, I understand why. The U.S. government was trying to shuttle as many civilians—American and South Vietnamese—out of there as quickly as possible.

On April 4, just a few weeks earlier, a C-5 carrying mostly orphans had crashed only minutes after leaving Tan Son Nhut, killing 138 people. For a time, the C-5 fleet was restricted, but as the rush to evacuate intensified, they were the only practical way out.

Within a day or two of my family leaving, the runways of Tan Son Nhut Airbase were so severely damaged by rocket fire that they were rendered unusable, and the desperate helicopter evacuations from the American embassy became the only way out of Saigon.

My family and our fellow refugees filled up the belly of the plane. I remember chewing bubble gum for the first time. I loved it! It tasted sweet, and I thought it was so nice of the soldiers to give us all gum. Later, I realized they gave us gum to help pop our ears at high altitudes.

We flew to Anderson Air Force Base, a military installation in Guam. We spent only one night in Guam before flying to America, but I remember that night. We were housed in barracks. They had to cram as many portable and bunk beds as they could into each building to handle our numbers. It was there that I had my one and only MRE, the military term for "meals ready to eat," prepackaged food for soldiers in the field. The boxes were made of thin, brown cardboard, and the rectangular trays had little slots in them for the various cans, which had pull tabs on top. The only thing I remember from that tray is the Vienna sausages. They were very tender and tasty, but I've never eaten them since. No particular reason, really; I just never have.

My sister, fifteen at the time, told me what she experienced there. In the barracks, we were overwhelmingly surrounded by fellow Vietnamese, so an American man stood out and caught her attention. She studied him intently. She saw tears running down his cheeks. Her compassion compelled her to approach him. She wanted to comfort him. When she asked him in her broken English why he was crying, he said he missed his wife. She wouldn't come with him to America because she wouldn't abandon her elderly mother, but she had given him custody of her two older children to bring them to America. His heart was aching; he feared he might never see her again.

Later that evening, this man asked my sister if she wanted to go somewhere on base, and she said yes. His request wasn't perverted; it was just for the company of somone who could speak English. My sister was just trying to be kind. They snuck away to a bar that evening and came back drunker than skunks.

I don't remember anything else until we arrived at Travis Air Force Base in northern California, and I remember only one thing there. When we walked out the exit door and descended the metal stairs, I was as cold as could be! Vietnam is a tropical country, and I had never experienced temperatures as chilly as an April day in California.

I'll explain all the events that culminated in my arrival in America in the next few chapters. I believe that if you understand all that had to occur for this to have happened, you too will see that it was nothing short of God's miraculous work.

CHAPTER THREE

BEFORE ME

Someone needs to tell those tales. When the battles are fought
and won and lost … someone needs to tell their bits
of overlapping narrative. There's magic in that.
It's in the listener, and for each and every ear it will be
different, and it will affect them in ways they can never
predict. From the mundane to the profound.
You may tell a tale that takes up residence in someone's soul,
becomes their blood and self and purpose.
—Erin Morgenstern, *The Night Circus*

Since I wanted this book to be my memoir, I hesitated about
telling my other family members' stories, but I realized that
everything that happens in a family becomes a part of each
member's story. Just because these events didn't happen to
me specifically doesn't mean they aren't a part of my life. We
are all creations of God; everything we do is full of signifi-
cance because he is preparing us for eternity.

My mother's oldest sister (Chi Hai) took on the role of mother in her life. Because Mom was the last of ten children from a truly poor, old woman, her mother and father didn't really bother with her. They didn't even give her a name. Chi Hai got her a birth certificate and named her. The Vietnamese name her sister gave to her, Mot, means something similar to "leftover trash." Her parents were very old—well past having children—so in her family's eyes, she was a leftover.

My mom was also given Chi Hai's husband's last name rather than her own father's last name. No one cared if her name was right or wrong, and throughout her childhood, kids made fun of her and beat her up because of her name. These people were just simple, uneducated and poor. Her other sister, Chi Ba, raised her the only way she knew how. She disciplined my mother often by beating her with thornbush twigs. It's no wonder she grew up with no sense of self-worth.

My mother told my sister what it was like growing up in a culture that prized boys over girls. She had been born into a family of eight other girls and one boy, and her parents worshiped him. They prepared a tray of food for him each day at dinner, and the family had to wait until he was done eating before they could eat the leftovers. One day, he didn't like the food, and he kicked it all over the room. That night, no one ate. He also often bullied my mother and made her do his homework and beat her often.

When she was older, my mother took judo lessons to learn to defend herself. She fell in love with the instructor and wanted to marry him. My mother's family disliked her fiancé and didn't want her to marry him. It was a tradition for the girl's family to invite the boy's relatives over for a family gathering for the asking of marriage. As the groom-to-be's family approached my mother's home, however, her parents sent dogs to chase them away. That shamed the groom's family.

Mom left home and went to live with her fiancé and married him. He was my mother's first husband, the father of my three oldest siblings. But because of the shame she had caused his family, they took turns verbally and physically abusing her. They turned her into their personal maid; she did all the cooking, cleaning, and laundry for the family.

Her father-in-law and her husband beat her more frequently than the other family members did. There were family rumors that my mother had even been raped by her father-in-law. The abuse continued until my mother started fighting back. When she finally pummeled her father-in-law, she left. Her husband gave her no reason to stay.

When she was pregnant with their first child, she had seen him kissing another woman down the street. She tried to kill herself by throwing herself into a deep well and drowning, but her instinct to survive wouldn't allow her to do that. That was the first time she tried to kill herself.

Mom took her first two children and went to live with another sister, Chi Nam. She was pregnant with her third child when she left. Mom rented a room from her sister and found work as a teacher; even though she was uneducated, she was well read. Mom had completed only seventh grade, but she was very intelligent and self-taught. Her husband came to get her and bring her home, but he got the hint when she threw a large knife at him.

My sister remembers life when it was just the three of them—Mom, Letty, and her brother, Canh. They were poor, but life was simple and calm. Shortly after Mom left her husband, they moved to a one-room shack on stilts over water. Mom had to work, so she paid her sister to babysit Canh. She couldn't afford to pay her to watch both children, so my mom, thinking Letty couldn't get into anything, left her at home all day. Letty remembers Mom's face being like that of a bright and beautiful angel. When Mom would leave for work, she would shut the door, and all the light disappeared. Letty was alone in darkness. She spent her days peeking through the slits between the floorboards and watching things pass by. She saw things like baby ducks, combs, money, and trash. When she later recounted this memory to my mother, Mom was shocked, as Letty was only ten months old at that time.

Soon, the third child arrived, my brother Ninh. Because multiple children would scare away any suitors, my mom kept her third child with her and sent Canh and Letty to live with the sister who had raised her, Chi Ba. Consistent in her methods, she beat Canh and Letty as she had beaten my mother. Canh was a very loving and kind brother who tried to protect Letty from punishment. In their teen years, however, he grew apart from her when he started doing drugs, which led him to become abusive toward her. This is behavior he learned from his father. He is not the same person he was then.

Mom later fell in love with Donald Lamb, a writer for the U.S. military who had a wife and children in the States. Donald was cultured and educated. He would take her ballroom dancing, and they became lovers. She became pregnant with her fourth. He loved my mother so much that he went AWOL (absent without leave) to spend time with her. When the MPs found him, they dragged him away while he kicked and screamed for her. She never saw him again.

Then, my mother met Jim. Talk about night and day. The polar opposite of Donald, Jim was a scrawny, tall, uncultured redneck from California. She married him because she was pregnant. I think there was another reason as well. After never being truly loved until she met Donald, an American, I think she was hoping for the same with Jim. Boy, was she wrong.

My mom kept her pregnancy a secret, so Jim thought Maurice was his son. She kept this to herself until she revealed it to him during one of their drunken fights. When my mom and dad first met, he was in the air force and operating radar. When he was discharged from the air force, they married, and he stayed in Vietnam. He couldn't get a job, so he got a degree in electronics by correspondence.

During the time he was working on a degree, he was unemployed, so they had no income. My mom and dad opened a bar and brothel because he had GI friends and she had friends in need. The girls my mom knew weren't established prostitutes; they were girls from educated families who were down on their luck because of the war. They were desperate for a way to survive and feed their families. The bar was on the first floor, and they used our bedrooms upstairs to run the prostitution side of the business.

One time, the police raided our home, and the prostitutes were rushed to the back of the house. At that time, our house had a cistern in the backyard from which water was pumped up into another tank on the roof and the gravity provided water to all areas of the home. These women were hidden in the cistern. My sister told me they were afraid one girl with a heart condition would die, but she didn't.

The next day, my mom went to the jail and bailed out all the girls who had been arrested. The neighbors soon got wind of what was going at our house, and they started cursing at my siblings when they walked by.

Once my dad finished his correspondence course and got a degree, he was able to get work, so they closed the bar and brothel. He got a job as vice president of ITT in Vietnam. He rubbed elbows with bigwigs such as Vietnamese and American generals. We had lots of money and became quite privileged. Times were so good that we even had paid household staff members. After my dad left, that all changed, but one nanny was so loyal to our family that she stayed on for six months without pay after he left.

But during that time of plenty, we enjoyed the benefits of wealth. My siblings and I attended the private International Vietnamese School with children of the well-to-do. Apparently, I became spoiled; my sister tells me I was a brat. I was stubborn, and even when I was being spanked, I'd scream and fight back. My siblings gave me the nickname Ba gia du, Vietnamese for "mean old lady." I didn't know that until recently, and I laughed because my sister could have been describing my older daughter, Michaela. When I told Michaela, we had a good chuckle.

Even though money wasn't a problem at that time, my dad missed his home in America. He'd get drunk and beat all the children and my mother. My sister remembers seeing him throw me across the room. Before I was born, he would drive his fist into my mother, kick her, and sit on her belly when she was pregnant. Jim would take a fistful of her hair and pound her head on the concrete floor of our home. I grew up not knowing why my mom suffered such horrific and debilitating migraines, but when I learned that, I understood.

When the police came—which was often—Dad would charm them, and they would leave, thinking nothing of the incident. He would disappear for days, and when he'd come home, he'd bring whatever STD he'd picked up with him.

My sister told me about one particular night she remembers; it was during the time when we had plenty. My mom loved art, and she had purchased and received many pieces that were still packed in crates. Well, that night, they got into a fight, and my dad beat my mother and broke every single crate and every piece of art my mother had bought. I could hear Letty choking back sobs as she retold this story forty-plus years later. She finished with, "I still remember watching him shoot at her as she ran up the stairs." The wall was riddled with bullet holes. I personally couldn't stay with an abuser. I understand why some women do it, but I certainly don't condone it.

My mother thought if she could make him feel at home, as if he were in America, he would be happy and want to stay. She knew that if he beat her in Vietnam, he'd beat her in America, but at least in Vietnam, she could speak the language and had some resources to help her. So she bought a Betty Crocker cookbook from Sears and tried to bake him an apple pie and other American dishes. My mother tried to make him happy.

It didn't work.

CHAPTER FOUR
MOMMA BEARS

For men are not cast off by the Lord forever.
Though he brings grief, he will show compassion,
so great is his unfailing love. For he does not willingly
bring affliction or grief to the children of men.
—Lamentations 3:31–33 NIV

A woman is like a tea bag. You never know how
strong she'll be until you put her in hot water.
—Eleanor Roosevelt

While conducting research for this chapter's title, I discovered researchers have found that mother bears rarely attack when their baby cubs are trapped. I found that pretty surprising—how about you? For now, I'll go with our stereotypical image of a massive mama bear standing on her hind legs, arms outstretched, claws and teeth bared, drool dripping from her fangs, and growling so loudly that your hair is blown back. All to protect her cub. How's that for an image, huh?

Well, that's how I see my mom now. It was only well after she died and I'd experienced life that I could understand and appreciate the sacrifices she made for me. No, she was no saint; however, she did what she had to so we could survive. I realize now that she did the best she could with what she had, and I'm no worse for the wear.

I have no idea how my mother did it all, but as I grow to know God more, I've found that his grace is new every day. He gives me what I need to get through whatever that day holds: "My grace is sufficient for you, for my strength is made perfect in weakness" (2 Corinthians 12:9 NIV).

I'm grateful for my sister as well. She didn't have to step up as a substitute mother, but she did. It was as God intended.

The day my father left, my mother had cooked dinner, and we sat at the table. As was customary, we weren't allowed to eat until he came home from work. We waited and waited at the table until late into the evening. He never came back. It was 1971, and I was two.

My mother tried to plan wisely with her finances. When times were good, she bought stock in a bank in Switzerland. She also had some money in a bank in Hawaii. When my father left, though, he took all the money we had.

To make matters worse, the Swiss broker embezzled all my mother's investments. Mom had to parent the six of us, alone, in a war-torn country with almost no resources.

After my father left, my mother became severely depressed and soon had a complete breakdown. She felt guilty for not having gone to America when Jim had asked her to. Some days, she didn't come out of her room. My oldest brother, Canh, began spending a lot of time at his friends' houses because they had food and creature comforts. So duty fell to the second oldest, my sister.

My sister got a very hard and fast shove from a part-time into a full-time mother role. Our house was the only resource we could liquidate, but Mom refused because she was afraid if Dad came back, he wouldn't know where to find us. Out of desperation, my sister sold what we had at a flea market—our clothes, pots and pans, paintings, purses, furniture—whatever she could. To stretch our money further, she'd wait at the market until almost all the booths were closed and make last-minute purchases in hopes that vendors would sell food cheaper just to get rid of it.

Once, we were so destitute that she picked up discarded grains of rice one at a time until she had enough for us to eat. For a time, this provided enough food for us and medicine for my mother's headaches.

During what I call the "brothel times" (after my dad left us), we had no income. Letty followed my aunt Chi Nam to help her sell jewelry. The brothels in the area were great locations to sell. In the brothels were girls her age. Most were orphans of the war, and men brought them to the brothels to sell them as slaves. Letty saw some of the prostitutes sending "helpers" to buy cigarettes for their clients. That's when the idea struck her. Letty removed the mirrored door from our medicine cabinet in the bathroom and used it as a classy tray for packs of cigarettes she'd buy and then sell at the doors of various brothels around town. She could speak French and English with the soldiers who frequented those establishments. That was Letty's daily life at age eleven.

As if it weren't hard enough raising four younger siblings, she also spent time fighting to keep my oldest brother, Canh, out of the house. She had to keep him from pilfering from our home things she could sell to buy food. In fits of anger, my brother would bang on every door and window and climb the balconies up to the third floor to try to get in. Letty was terrified of him.

Eventually, our water was shut off, and the kerosene delivery was stopped as well, so we had no water or fuel for cooking. Then one day, Letty noticed something strange on a wooden shelf in the living room. When she poked at it with her finger, it disintegrated. Termites were eating the wooden furniture and doors in our house, so she decided to use the wood to fuel the fires to cook outside on our terrace.

When my mother finally came out of her deep depression, she made money by renting out rooms in our house. She also did heavy manual labor. In an effort to reduce the forest so the enemy couldn't hide, the U.S. military sprayed napalm on the forests in Vietnam. Water boils at around 200 degrees Fahrenheit, but napalm burns at 1,500 to 2,000 degrees. This tactic left acres of standing but charred trees. My mother recruited one man to go for three days at a time into battlefields and harvest the charred trees, which had been turned into charcoal, to bring back and sell. My mother was just four foot eleven, and she weighed 100 pounds at the time and she only had hand saws. I'm a bit taller and have 50-plus pounds on her, but when I cut wood with my husband for two hours, I'm beat! I cannot fathom what that did to her body and spirit.

My mother had noticed in passing an adoption agency near the market. It meant nothing to her until my father left. The office was working with the Pearl S. Buck Foundation, founded by the American author Pearl S. Buck, whose parents had been missionaries in China. Buck had a heart for unwanted children, especially children of Asian cultures. Pearl had founded the agency in 1949, but it didn't open offices in Asia until the mid-1960s. Pearl coined the term *Amerasian,* and she became outraged that children of mixed races were considered unadoptable.

Long before it was considered fashionable or politically correct, Buck challenged the American public by raising consciousness on topics such as racism, sex discrimination, and the plight of the thousands of babies born to Asian women left behind and unwanted wherever American soldiers were based in Asia.

The Buck Foundation was a key player in Operation Babylift, the same operation that President Ford authorized starting on April 3, 1975. The last flight of evacuated orphans went out on April 26, 1975. Jerry Qui, a Vietnamese refugee who helped orphanage workers load babies onto the last flight out of Saigon, remembered the panic of the final days. Thousands crowded around the gates of the orphanage as buses left for the airport. He frantically helped workers load babies into grocery-store boxes and strap them into the plane with cargo belts. The pilot, worried about being shot down, took off vertically. "All the babies on the floor piled up," Qui recalled. "It looked like a mountain at the end of the tail [of the plane]." Bob Zwier, an air force medic who flew on several of the babylifts, remembers planes so crowded with children that the crew had to unload food to get off the ground. Most of the children were ill and got sick on the flight. "The heat and the stench, that sticks with you forever," Zwier said.[1]

Being so destitute and so sad, my mom considered giving us up for adoption. One morning, she told Letty to gather all the kids because we were all walking to the market. When Letty asked why, my mother was very honest with her. "I'm going to give you all away so you can have a better life."

My sister burst into tears that streamed down her face the whole way there. She, the four of us younger children, and my mother made our way to the adoption agency. My mom instructed Letty to take us to the courtyard to play while she talked to the woman in the office. The rest of us, of course, were oblivious to what was going on. Letty told me later that Mom didn't want to do it, but she knew why Mom was thinking about it. If we were provided for, she could kill herself. My mother was filled with such a depth of sorrow and hopelessness that she saw that as a way out.

1 articles.philly.com/2005-04-08/news/25426524_1_children-with-adoptive-families-vietnamese-children-private-adoption-agencies.

When Mom finally came out of the office, she said they could place only the three youngest; no one wanted to adopt older kids. My mom said it was all the kids or none. Had they taken us all, my mother would have died soon thereafter, but that wasn't God's plan.

Since giving us up for adoption was no longer an option, my mother rented a place and started another bar and brothel. That kept us fed for a short time until my mother ran out of money. She rented another place and made a third attempt, but that failed quickly as well.

She had run out of ideas for how to feed us and had lost all sense of self-worth. She began prostituting herself. She brought customers to our home, and many of them beat her. The neighbors knew what Mom was doing. Some of the neighborhood men would come on to her, and that made her angry. It was a job to her, separate from being a neighbor, but the neighbors didn't see it that way. I think that was the only way she was able to keep an ounce of pride and not hate herself completely.

During that time, she became pregnant an estimated ten times. My sister accompanied her to abortion after abortion; my mother suffered from an irregular heartbeat and nonstop hemorrhaging at times. The abortion clinics were back-alley, coat-hanger facilities. On several occasions, my mother passed out on the way home due to blood loss, and my sister had to get help. My sister begged her to sell the house so we could have money. She resisted until she couldn't take the beatings any longer.

When Mom finally acquiesced and sold the house, we had lots of money. She rented a nice house and told Letty to buy furniture, decorate it, and make it a home. Letty did so gladly. Letty began drawing and painting. About that time, my brother Canh came back to live with us and antagonized her by drawing on her artwork or vandalizing it. One time, she ate one of her drawings before he could get to it. When he started to beat her, she began screaming as if she were crazy. That intimidated Canh enough to stop him.

She'd discovered a way to defend herself, but she took it too far. She screamed for hours. For fear that she might run away, my mother and Canh locked Letty in her room for days. When that didn't change anything, they took her to a mental institution. The doctor looked in her eyes and told her what he saw. "I can see something very painful in your eyes. But you have to deal with it because if you get stuck in here, you'll become crazy and never leave."

She prayed all night for a sign from God. If she acted crazy, her brother wouldn't beat her. But if she continued acting crazy, she'd be institutionalized. In the middle of the night, she had a seizure and was taken to the hospital. When the seizure finally stopped, she considered what had happened. The seizure was the answer she was seeking from God. He had shown her what it was like to be sick—for real. She stopped acting crazy.

Ironically, now we (my sister, my kids, my husband, and I) joke about "Crazy Aunti Nuet" all the time and laugh about it. (Nuet is her Americanized name, short for her birth name, Nguyet.)

CHAPTER FIVE

BITTERSWEET

Love your neighbor as yourself.
—Leviticus 19:18 NIV

Since 1971, when I was two, my mom had parented the six of us alone. With my sister's help, she worked very hard every day to keep us from starving. At times, all we had was rice to make soup. We lived in the city, but we didn't have much to do.

Letty used to hang out at a pool to which she'd take me at times. I was about five when we met Melody Woodson there. Melody's father, Woody Woodson, was a civilian working for the U.S. government in Vietnam. Melody and her mother, Sarah Woodson, had come to visit Mr. Woodson for the summer. Melody was nine, close to my sister's age, about eleven. She thought I was adorable, and she began a conversation with Letty. Theirs eventually developed into a long friendship.

And Sarah was happy to have a playmate for her daughter. She was a very kind, Christian woman. She fed us that first day and then offered to drive us home. She became aware of our situation when she dropped us off at our big house with no lights on. Our water and electricity were off due to our financial situation. She asked to meet our parents, but my sister told her that our mother was "not well." Mrs. Woodson insisted, so Letty called Mom outside. When Mom came out, Mrs. Woodson could see she looked a bit off. The effects of the daily struggles, the migraines, and the depression were visible on my mother's face. After Mom went back inside, Letty explained that my father had abandoned us and that we were struggling.

Being such a compassionate soul, Mrs. Woodson started bringing us some daily basic supplies such as bread, milk, and peanut butter as well as a few treats including cookies. She came every day, and one day, she told Letty, "Things aren't right in your life. Your life would be better with God." Sarah explained to my sister God's plan of salvation, and Letty received Christ that day. Letty was so desperate to believe in something that would enable her to survive. It gave her hope.

They told my mom, and she wanted to be saved that day as well. Mrs. Woodson took us to church at the First Assembly of God every Sunday until she left Vietnam. It was there that all the newly saved attendees were driven to the beach in a bus and baptized. My whole family was baptized that day. I don't think any of us understood what it all meant. In fact, I didn't know any of this until I was in my forties.

When the time came for Melody and her mother to go home, Mrs. Woodson asked her friend Vivian Clark to keep an eye on us. Mrs. Woodson and Mrs. Clark attended the First Assembly of God, and Mrs. Clark worked as a secretary for the American embassy. Mrs. Clark was kind to us also; she often showed her love though simple acts such as baking a cake for each of us kids on our birthdays. We visited her home often; we walked with Letty about an hour each way to receive this kindness. This was so special for us, as no one ever showed us this type of kindness.

Because Mrs. Clark worked for the embassy, she was privy to the status of the war. One day, she told Letty, "I have a secret to tell you. If you come here one day to visit and I'm not here, that means I had to go home. I may not have a chance to say good-bye to you. When the Americans pull out of Vietnam, they'll have to do it secretly. I'll try my best to let you know when."

A few weeks later, we made the hour-long walk to Mrs. Clark's home. She was gone. Letty knew we had to get out of Vietnam. She was just fifteen, but she begged Mom, "If they've bombed the presidential palace, what makes you think they won't kill the kids? If you don't leave, I'm leaving without you!"

My mom knew Letty was a huge help in her life, and Letty knew that too. Letty used that as leverage to help convince our mother to flee to America. It worked. That was in April 1975.

Following through on her promise to help take care of us, Mrs. Clark had made a verbal request that her church, National Evangelical Free Church in Annandale, Virginia, sponsor my family and bring us to America. That was before she left Vietnam. Understandably, the responsibility of bringing a family of seven to America was a daunting task; the church members felt it was too great of an obligation for them to take on and decided not to do it.

But before Vivian Clark was evacuated from the American embassy and stepped on a plane for home, she wrote a second request, asking her church to reconsider its decision. Her simple act of caring was such a powerful expression of God's compassion for my family.

Vivian Clark never made it home. Her plane was shot down by Communist gunfire. A C-5A Galaxy cargo plane flew the initial mission of Operation Babylift to bring Vietnamese orphans to the United States in the last remaining days before the Republic of Vietnam fell.

The C-5 departed from Saigon–Tan Son Nhut Airbase on April 4, 1975, just before four in the afternoon. Twelve minutes after takeoff, an apparent explosion tore apart the lower rear fuselage. The locks of the rear-loading ramp failed, causing the door to open and separate; rapid decompression occurred. The crew managed to keep control of the plane for a short time. They descended and prepared to land back in the town of Tan Son Nhat.

About halfway through a turn to final approach, the plane dropped rapidly. Unable to make it to the runway at Tan Son Nhut Airbase, the pilot tried to bring the nose up. The C-5 touched down in a rice paddy. It skidded for a quarter-mile. The aircraft became airborne again for a half-mile before hitting a dike and breaking into four parts, some of which caught fire. Killed in the crash were 138 people, including 78 children and 35 Defense Attaché Office Saigon personnel.[2] Vivian Clark was one.

When the news of Vivian's death reached her church, its members prepared for her funeral. On the day of her me-

---

2 en.wikipedia.org/wiki/1975_Tan Son Nhut C-5_accident.

morial service, her final letter arrived. Pastor Gerald Hall read the letter aloud to the congregation. They considered her letter to be her dying wish. They respected it, and agreed to bring my family to America.

I have no words to adequately express my gratitude to Vivian Clark for her simple act of kindness. It forever changed my life. If she could explain this now, I believe she would simply say, "I was doing what God wanted me to do."

People have no idea how meaningful even small acts of kindness and compassion can be and how deep a mark they can leave on others' lives. I've used this story as an example when I talk to others about God. The same question comes up every time: "Why does God let bad things happen to good people?" I can't give them a definitive answer, but just as Jesus used parables to help people understand, I tell them this story. If Mrs. Clark hadn't died, I wouldn't be here, in America.

My mom started working on all the necessary paperwork to get our passports. She collected all the money she had and filled a briefcase with it. When she finally received all the passports, my mother and five of us children took a cab to the American embassy, where we boarded a bus to the airport. My brother Canh was nowhere to be found. The bus would transport only family members of Americans, and since three of us kids had passports indicating that we were U.S. citizens, we all qualified.

The bus dropped us off at the airport, and while we awaited instructions, Mom started to cry. She said she couldn't leave her oldest son. She left the airbase, risking the possibility that she wouldn't get back through the military checkpoint.

She used the cash she had to bribe everyone to find Canh. She found him, but they couldn't get back inside the airbase. They walked a little ways away. Then, as a diplomat's limousine was leaving the checkpoint, my mom threw herself in front of it. She opened the briefcase, revealing all the money, and offered it to the driver if he would get them through the checkpoint. He agreed. Mom and Canh hid in the back, lying on the floor. They sailed right in, and shortly thereafter, we were herded onto a C-5 cargo bound for Guam.

While we were in Guam, the American Red Cross helped us by attempting to contact any connections we had in America to take us in once we arrived in the United States. They called my dad's family. His sister, Lauralee, said no. His father said no. Letty told them to contact Mrs. Woodson. Mrs. Woodson said yes, but since she was a housewife with no income, they would need her husband to agree and sign the papers. She begged and pleaded with him, but he refused. Mrs. Woodson contacted her church, but it also declined.

As a last resort, Mrs. Woodson called Vivian Clark's church. She hadn't received news of Vivian's death and wasn't aware she was calling on the day of her memorial service. She made the request, and the church said yes. After Pastor Hall read Vivian's letter, everyone put money into the collection plate to pay for our airfare from California to Virginia. Ruben Johnson, a deacon at the church, signed the papers that committed him to taking responsibility for our large family.

National Evangelical Free Church of Annandale, Virginia, took us in—all seven of us. Pastor Hall and his wife welcomed us to their small parsonage and fed and clothed us. Because no one wanted to rent to a single mother with six children, the church had to buy a house. The congregation found a house down the street from the church, and Mr. Johnson bought the house in his own name. Though we had government assistance (Section 8 housing funds) to help to pay for it, I know he didn't profit a dime from doing that; he did it out of sheer kindness. And, boy, were we rough on that house.

The extreme circumstances of our immigration have given me such a sense of gratitude for America and a deeply grateful heart for our American soldiers. Those who served in Vietnam fought the war out of their sense of duty and got nothing but disrespect and hatred in return. They gave their lives for so many, including me, and I still thank every Vietnam Vet I meet.

When I was a child, I looked noticeably Asian, and because of that, though I'm a U.S. citizen, I remember feeling there was something wrong with me—as if I were always an outsider. The kids treated me differently, and no one wanted to be my friend.

God allowed me to use these feelings to cultivate compassion for the outcast much as Vivian Clark and the people of National Evangelical Free Church showed compassion for my family. Their examples of love encourage me to this day and have shaped my dreams for my life. I owe a debt to the church and its members, a debt I can never repay. Ultimately, at the root of the church's kindness and compassion was its faith in God, who told us, "Love thy neighbor as thyself."

*Sarah Woodson (left)
and Melody Woodson with
daughter on her lap.*

CHAPTER SIX

A WHOLE NEW WORLD—
TROUBLE IN PARADISE

Toto, I've a feeling we're not in Kansas anymore.
—Dorothy, *The Wizard of Oz*

Ever jumped into a really cold pool? You know that initial shock that rushes over you? That's what I felt when we stepped off the plane at Travis Air Force Base in northern California. The average temperature when we left Vietnam in April was about ninety-five; the temperature when we arrived was in the fifties. *Brrrrr!*

Since we didn't know how long we were going to be at the base, my sister once again went into supply mode. Letty dove into some clothing bins and pulled out duds of every size and gender for us all. Next, she went in search of supplies and food. On her way, she saw a holly tree with beautiful, bright-red berries and decided she had to have a taste. Fortunately, she had only a few and moved on. One or two holly berries are harmless, but twenty or so can be fatal.

Letty was an independent, adventurous child, and in her search for more supplies, she walked right off the base! She realized it was Sunday, and she remembered seeing in American movies people sticking out their thumbs at passing cars to catch rides. A woman in a truck picked her up and asked, "Where are you going?"

"Church!" Letty said.

"Which one?"

"Any church!"

"Oh, you can come with me then."

The kind woman drove Letty to her church and sat with her through the service. When the speaker asked if there were any new guests there, Letty stood up proudly. When she was asked where she was from, she replied, "Vietnam."

"And when did you arrive?"

"Today," she said.

Of course, everyone was surprised and was very kind and welcoming. They insisted she come to brunch at the home of one of the church members. Being the free spirit she was, she went. Though it was her first day in a strange new country, her attitude was, "Sure! Why not?"

At the brunch, the homeowners offered Letty a horseback ride, and she jumped right on. After an afternoon of food and riding, Letty was invited to another function, a birthday party. Once again, she was ready to go, but she wanted to change her clothes before the party, so the kind woman in the truck gave her a ride back to the base.

When she arrived, she heard over the loudspeaker, "Please be on the lookout for a lost Vietnamese girl. She's about five feet tall—" Letty thought, *Hey! They're talking about me, but I'm not lost!* Apparently, everyone was frantically searching for her because she was holding up the flight to Virginia! Everyone was so upset, but she couldn't understand why since she had just wanted to go to church.

Letty's life hasn't changed much. If you talk to her, you'll find that adventures like that happen to her regularly even though she's no longer new to American life.

Mr. Rueben Johnson picked us up at Dulles Airport in Virginia and took us to his home. My sister can recall his suburban neighborhood. The streets were clean, the people were happy, and they dressed so nicely. Everyone had a big home and a manicured yard of lush, green grass. She said it was like a Thomas Kinkade painting. The sun was shining, the trees and plants were in bloom, and Mr. Johnson had beautiful flowers in his backyard. It was a peaceful paradise.

Letty was entranced by the beauty around her; it was

such a sharp contrast to the life she had been living. On the day we arrived, she saw a bicycle in the backyard and asked Mr. Johnson if she could ride it. "Of course you can," he said. "Just no farther than the end of the street, okay?" Based on what I've told you about my sister, you can guess something crazy was about to happen, right?

In Vietnam, small towns were quite close to each other, so it was common to ride a bike from town to town. Letty rode around the neighborhood for a while, and then she rode out of the subdivision onto a more heavily traveled road. She had corresponded with Mrs. Woodson and knew she lived in Fairfax, Virginia. Letty stopped several times to ask directions to Fairfax. Eventually, she found herself on the Beltway, that massive highway that loops around Washington. At that time, the Beltway was four or five lanes in each direction in parts, and recently, it's become nine to ten lanes each way.

My sister said she rode the bike all day. People honked and yelled at her. She thought they were just being mean, but that didn't bother her. It never occurred to her that she was the only bicyclist on the highway; she just kept pedaling.

It was only when it began to get dark that she decided to get off the highway. She exited and rode to a house, knocked on the door, and asked for help. She gave them Mrs.

Woodson's name and address. Fortunately, Mrs. Woodson was listed in the phonebook. Anyone remember phonebooks? Thick books with really thin pages? My, how times have changed. Mrs. Woodson came for Letty and returned her to Mr. Johnson's house. Everyone thought Letty had been kidnapped. No one even considered that she could have purposely ridden off on an adventure.

We lived with Pastor Gerald Hall, his wife, Vivian, and his daughter, Ann. Their son, John, was grown and out of the house. Poor Ann; she must have been overwhelmed by our strange family. Their home had only two bedrooms; they had prepared an attic room for us.

One time, my mother saw Ann up in a tree in the backyard. When my mother asked Mrs. Hall why Ann was up there, Mrs. Hall said that Ann wasn't used to all the noise and so many people, so she had climbed the tree to get away from the kids. A few days later, Mrs. Hall looked up and saw my mom in the tree. When Mrs. Hall asked her why, she gave her the same response: "To get away from the kids." I know many mothers who can identify with that.

Mrs. Hall told me years later that the first few days were interesting. She would find us lying on the floor all around the house because of the jet lag and the big time difference we were adjusting to. When we were tired, we just lay down and slept wherever. She said she felt as though she was walking through a minefield as she carefully stepped over our bodies.

Mrs. Hall first had to measure our waists to buy us all underwear; apparently, we didn't wear any. She was surprised to find that our waist sizes were all the same. That may have been due to the fact we were all a bit malnourished. For breakfast, she cooked rice for us, assuming it was what we commonly ate. In an ironic twist, however, her daughter wanted the rice with milk and sugar on it and we ate Corn Flakes. We'd eaten cereal before but not often; it was expensive, and we considered it a treat.

A few years ago, when I visited the Halls, Mrs. Hall told me a funny story about my family. My brother Ninh had a great sense of humor and would joke around with Mrs. Hall about eating her cat. Of course, Mrs. Hall knew he was only kidding and never took him seriously. We had been in the States for a few months when she and Pastor Hall attended a conference out of town. While they were gone, sadly, their cat was run over by a car. My brother immediately panicked; he was scared Mrs. Hall would assume the worst—that we had eaten it! He put the dead cat in a box so he could prove we hadn't. When their son, John, came to check on us, we told him what had happened. He urged us to bury the cat in the backyard as the carcass was starting to stink. John called Mrs. Hall, and though she was saddened by the cat's death, she had to laugh.

Mrs. Hall was amazingly gracious in giving her time to help us. Consider that she was accustomed to caring for only her husband and daughter and then all of a sudden she was cooking, cleaning, and doing laundry for seven more.

She was also responsible for enrolling all the children in school. The pile of paperwork was mountainous, and then we had to get immunizations before we could start school, so she hauled us to the doctor and the social service offices. Being a mother of four and having been a foster parent (talk about paperwork!), I have great appreciation for all Vivian Hall did to help us. Not everyone is so willing to share his or her time and personal space, which are precious personal commodities.

We lived with the Halls for several months before moving into the house Rueben Johnson had purchased for us to live in. My mother's English was pretty good, but she didn't have a grasp of American culture, so when the church members told her they were going to give her a shower for the new home, she cried. She thought they wanted to bathe her because she was dirty or smelled bad. Everyone had a good laugh after it was explained to Mom.

It was in that home that I had many of my first experiences. We had arrived in April, so we didn't experience our first winter until seven or eight months later. Because we had come from a tropical country that was hot all year round, we considered snow an amazing thing—the only plus when it comes to cold weather.

I was in the living room one day when I noticed something falling in slow motion outside. I was mesmerized by the strange sight. Even though I'd been attending school for months, I hadn't been taught about snow. It was something everyone there took for granted, of course.

I stepped out onto the front porch, stuck my hand out, and watched as each flake landed and melted. The sky was full of snowflakes. I remember thinking how beautiful it was. Seeing the ground covered with fresh, clean snow took my breath away. I came to love playing in the snow. It didn't matter that it froze my feet and hands. It didn't matter if I hadn't eaten all day because I'd been playing in the snow. I was surprised to learn that snow was rain in another form. It was simply magical to me, just like Christmas.

That first Christmas hooked me for the rest of my life. There's no more wonderful time of year for me than Christmas. My kids complain when I start playing Christmas music at the end of October. I listen to it nonstop in the kitchen, in the car, in the bedroom. I love everything about it: the cold, the music, the decorations, the lights, the tree, and the gift giving.

December 1975 was my first Christmas. We had a fireplace, and just sitting by the fire gave me such a warm and fuzzy feeling. We hung stockings on the mantel, but I had no idea why. The lights on the tree were dazzling, and the mood was festive. I had no idea what was going on around me that gave me that feeling. The only time we had like that in Vietnam was the New Year's celebration; we would receive gifts then and on our birthdays. But even the decorations for the New Year celebration in Vietnam couldn't compare with Christmas decorations.

I woke up early on Christmas morning and ran to the tree. I thought everyone had lied about Santa because I saw nothing under the tree! My mom came into the living room, where all of us kids were running around, and she opened the front door. There they were—the presents! Mom explained that Santa couldn't come down the chimney because of the fire, so he had left all the presents on the front porch. I don't remember if I got anything else that year, but I'll never forget the pink sleeping bag. I'd never had one, and until I was thirty-three, that was the only one I ever had. I loved that sleeping bag.

Now that I'm older, Christmas has a much deeper, more serious meaning to me, of course. My elation is mixed with sorrow and sometimes guilt knowing Christ was born to suffer and die so I would be saved from eternity in hell. For this, I am so grateful.

My first time away from home and my family was the following summer, in 1976. The church sent my two youngest brothers and me to Camp Orchard Hill in Pennsylvania. It was a long bus ride, especially for a kid who suffered from motion sickness, but I loved that camp and its bunk beds and lots of fun activities. I rode horses, did arts and crafts, and discovered new foods such as oatmeal with milk and sugar. It was there that I was saved.

A group of us kids were sitting around the campfire one night listening to a counselor explain God's plan of salvation. For some reason, I felt rebellious; I started running around the campfire to avoid the counselor's question, "Do you want to be saved?" When she finally caught me, we sat down and prayed together. I didn't understand what I had done, but I see now that the seed had been planted then.

That seed hibernated for about seventeen years before it began to sprout because life had hardened my heart. It was another ten years before that seed began to grow, and another seven years before it blossomed. The fact that my progression took so long is something I regret, but I trust that was God's plan and that he knew I wasn't ready to truly serve him until then. I still had (and have) a lot to learn and experience.

You've heard, "It takes a village to raise a child." Well, it took an entire congregation to raise my family. In addition to Rueben Johnson and Pastor Hall and his wife, many other members of the church cared for us. Paul and Lucille Nylander acted like parents to my mom. They gave her spiritual guidance and money when we were in dire straits. Even though my mom worked as an electronic board assembler and went to school at Control Data Institute, we found it hard to make ends meet. Some of the church members weren't able to sacrifice so much of their time, but they did what they could. Some babysat or brought their children to play with us to help us acclimate and practice our English. They truly lived Matthew 25:40 NIV: "Whatever you did for the least of these brothers and sisters of mine, you did it for me."

At times, assimilating wasn't easy, but at other times, it seemed some things were universal. Take teenagers, for instance. The church made sure my mother had driving lessons so she could obtain a driver's license. They gave us an older car so she could drive to work. We all know cars in the sixties tended to be big, but this car was huge even by the standards of that day. It was a tank, but Canh, who was seventeen then, and Letty, who was fifteen, thought it was really cool.

One day, they decided to take it for a spin. Of course, Canh didn't have a license. They waited until my mom was asleep and snuck the keys out of her purse. They put the car in neutral and let it roll out of the driveway so they wouldn't wake my mother when they started it.

The joy part of the joyride ended in Falls Church, Virginia. Neither of them had any concept of speed limits. Canh was driving fifty or sixty in a residential neighborhood with narrow streets and cars parked on both sides when he slammed into the back of a station wagon. He was stunned when it happened; Letty had to slap his face to bring him out of his mesmerized state. My sister tells me that in Vietnam, when you did something like that, the owner would come out of his home and beat you to death. That was their fear.

She screamed at Canh, "Let's go! Get out of here! Go!"

They drove home and devised a plan. Truly afraid that mom was going to kill them, Letty told Canh, "Mom wouldn't kill us in front of Pastor Hall, so let's call him and he can tell her." In the middle of the night, Canh called Pastor Hall and explained what had happened—but he left out the part about Letty being with him; Letty had convinced him that it wasn't necessary to mention that.

Pastor Hall came over, woke up my mom, and filled her in on the evening's events. Pastor Hall and Canh traced his route back to the damaged car and left a note on the windshield. The church ended up paying for the damages, but no charges were filed.

Canh eventually got his license, but he continued to speed. In the end, he acquired enough tickets to have his license suspended. He continued to drive on a suspended license, so a warrant was issued for his arrest. The church posted bail, but he jumped bail and took off for California. I often wondered if anyone—Pastor Hall, Mrs. Hall, any member of that church—ever asked themselves, *What have we gotten ourselves into?*

CHAPTER SEVEN
POVERTY AND PUPPY LOVE

We think sometimes that poverty is only
being hungry, naked and homeless.
The poverty of being unwanted, unloved
and uncared for is the greatest poverty.
—Mother Teresa

When you're poor, an awful shame follows you around like a dark cloud. The strange thing was I didn't know we were poor until I ate lunch at school in America. I don't remember who said what or even what was said, but I remember we had green lunch tickets because we were on welfare. We'd give the tickets to the lunch lady, who would punch a hole in them every time we got lunch.

Everyone else paid cash or brought a lunch lovingly packed for them by their moms. I became ashamed and embarrassed about the lunch tickets because they made it so obvious to our classmates we were on welfare, and kids can be cruel. They pointed at us and whispered to each other. They looked down on us. If our worn, second-hand clothes weren't enough to give us away, that lunch ticket certainly was.

I eventually stopped eating lunch altogether and acted as if I weren't hungry. I would rather go hungry than be looked down upon. There was never much food to eat in our house, so I didn't eat breakfast either. Many nights, dinner consisted of Ramen noodle soup.

I find this all too ironic. I'd come from a Third World country where I was malnourished and hungry most of the time. There I was in America, the land of plenty, being offered free food but choosing to starve myself. It was so important for me to fit in that I was willing to go hungry to be more acceptable to people I didn't even know. Isn't that crazy?

I'm still amazed at how shame and poverty go hand in hand and at the indelible mark poverty leaves on one's life. However, it's shaped my character and added to my pool of compassion. As painful as it was, I wouldn't change a thing; having been poor has taught me to appreciate all I have. I don't cherish what I have; my possessions aren't my number-one priority in life, but I do appreciate what I'm given, and I have a grateful heart. A plaque on my wall says it perfectly: "I ask God for all things that I might enjoy life. He gave me life that I might enjoy all things."

I also look on that part of my life as a pivotal time when God molded and prepared me for what was to come. Poverty can break you, certainly, but it can also be a powerful tool that can teach you humility, kindness, and compassion. Poverty can also make you strong and aggressive, and these are great assets when you face life's challenges. I thank God for the bad things as well as the good; both had such a profound effect on my life.

The lack that I had experienced in a Third World country contrasted sharply with the plenty I found in America. I have immense gratitude for every little thing. I feel I've become a better steward of what God gives me. I may enjoy shopping, for instance, but I won't spend $50 on a purse when a $20 one will suffice.

My children, however, have grown up in America. A conversation I had with my son drove this point home. He and I had watched a story about a floating bed that cost $1 million. He said with some seriousness that if he had a billion dollars, he'd buy one. I could never do that. So many people could benefit from that $1 million that I'd feel terribly guilty spending it on a floating bed.

Similarly, I could buy a new car, but I love driving my twelve-year-old minivan. I'm so grateful my children have been blessed to grow up in America, but I know my childhood has resulted in an abundance of humility, which has grown my spiritual life and has encouraged me to serve others. It has also given me perspective as to what is important in life.

Growing up poor made me strong; I knew I had to work hard and fight for everything. I've taught my children that, and they've seen it in their parents. Our hard work has paid off on many occasions, but I don't allow that to make me forget it's God who opens doors and gives me opportunities that I could never make for myself.

The shame of being poor and not having new clothes made me feel ugly. I didn't receive affection at home, nor did I receive any reassurance. I didn't have friends, so I played with my brothers. I was the classic tomboy. If you look at the few photos I have of me when I was nine or ten, you could just tell. I even *looked* like a boy.

When I expressed my disappointment with myself, my mom told me the story of the ugly duckling who one day turned into a beautiful swan. As stupid as it sounds, that story gave me hope. It's normal for a girl to want to feel pretty. I think I equated beauty with love somehow; I wanted affection—I wanted to be loved, something I felt was missing in my life until sixth grade.

Being loved gives you a sense of security, and I had none at that time. I didn't feel loved because my mom was never there. In retrospect, I know she was never there because she was working and going to school to better our lives, but I didn't understand that at the time. My dad wasn't part of my life, and I wasn't close to my siblings. And when my mom was there, her mental illness made her emotionally and physically unavailable. She would sleep for days sometimes or just stay in her room. Back then, I didn't understand or care why she was like that; she just was. I didn't know a mom was supposed to be any different. It may have been from head trauma or her bi-polar disorder or both. I have inherited her bipolar condition; I see the situation now through the clear lens of experience.

I always felt I had to be tough to keep up with my older brothers since I was the baby. All that changed for me in sixth grade. Many elementary schools in the area were closing and sending their students elsewhere. My elementary school closed after I finished fifth grade. Starting a new elementary school was very hard, but it was one of those moments in my life I'll always cherish because the ugly duckling became the swan.

Sebastian was a French boy in my class. His parents had been born and raised in France. I thought he was the best-looking boy in my class. He had a round face, brown hair, and beautiful, blue eyes. He spoke French fluently. Because he was tough and well-liked by the other kids, no one messed with him.

I played a lot of dodgeball in school and at home. Because I was the smallest, I had learned to be quick or my brothers would pelt me with that little red rubber ball. Anyone who has ever played dodgeball knows the ball can leave welts. By sixth grade, I was pretty good at dodgeball. Sebastian loved to play the game; he was a great predator. He used to wind up the ball before he threw it; he'd cup it in his wrist and spin around a couple times before whipping it at an unsuspecting victim. No one knew who it would be because he wouldn't look at anyone specifically as he spun around. No one knew when he was gonna let it go. When we picked teams for dodgeball, he always chose me. He never teased or picked on me, not even jokingly.

I don't know when it happened, but I fell in love with him. I know now it was puppy love, but, man, did I fall hard. He was always kind to me; he even told me one time that I was the prettiest girl he'd ever met. I loved to listen to him speak to his parents in French. I started strutting more like a peacock and less like an ugly duckling. Knowing that he liked me gave me a sense of self-worth and confidence. The cutest, toughest boy in the class liked me! I wanted to wear more dresses and act more like a girl, but he didn't care what I wore because he liked me for me. He didn't care I was a poor refugee from Vietnam.

We spent a lot of time at his house. His parents owned a restaurant in Washington. They were the nicest people I'd ever met. I don't remember his dad much, but I'll never forget his mom, Marie. She was a very sweet woman. She always fed me when I came over. She talked to me and was always interested in me.

Wherever Sebastien is, I hope he's happy. He deserves that and more. His simple act of being kind changed me from awkward and shy to outgoing and more confident. Don't get me wrong; I was still insecure. Nothing was stable in my life. With only one parent, I was always looking over my shoulder, waiting for the moment when I would become an orphan.

We all have a need to feel secure, and part of that requires our feeling that we fit in. That feeling was so strong that by eighth grade I had started hanging out with the only kids who would accept me. I didn't fit in with the jocks and cheerleaders or with the preppy rich kids. I didn't come from money or have the most stylish clothes. I wasn't a smart nerd, so I gravitated to the kids who accepted just about everyone, the "freaks" who smoked, skipped school, and did drugs.

My home life was nonexistent, and I simply didn't feel loved. I don't blame my mother; she did the best she could. She seemed to always be working or sleeping. All my siblings were off doing their own things, and I began to party on weekends. Though I got in with a bad crowd, my grades were very good until my senior year. Strangely, I was still responsible; I did all my homework and got a job. I was just thirteen, but I lied about that and got a job as a cashier at McDonalds. I began buying my own food and clothes. I also gave my mom money for rent from time to time when she ran short.

So I was unsupervised, and I had some income. That was a dangerous combination. At fourteen, I was drinking heavily and smoking marijuana as well as cigarettes—all to be cool and fit in. I became wild; I came and went as I pleased and did whatever I wanted. I spent entire weekends at friends' or boyfriends' houses. There was a party every weekend; somebody's parents would be out of town or an older friend of a friend would have his own place where anything was game.

By age fifteen, I was wearing skimpy minidresses with four-inch heels and going barhopping with friends in Georgetown using fake IDs. We wanted to get drunk and dance. We'd hitch rides with friends or split cab fare, party until two in the morning, and go home with people we barely knew. It was a miracle I didn't get mugged or beaten and left for dead in a dark alley during those days. When I think back to that time in my life, I'm more grateful than ever for the undeserved gift of God's protection over me.

My memories of that time sadden me. I was such a mess. No matter how much fun I thought I was having, I always felt unhappy but couldn't understand why. If I could speak to that little girl, I'd tell her that drugs and alcohol wouldn't replace her father or fill the void of loneliness and sorrow in her family life, that she would still feel empty. I'd introduce her to the only one who could fill that void and give her real joy. That desire lives deep in me; it's what drives me to run our youth ranch.

*I'm the one on the left
(age eight) who looks
like a boy.*

*My kindergarten
school picture, 1975*

CHAPTER EIGHT
DRIVING MISS CRAZY

When you're dead, you don't know you're dead.
You don't feel anything.
It's the people around you who suffer.
It's the same when you're stupid.
—A funeral director

I wish this were true about mental illness—blissful ignorance. Sometimes, people don't know they're suffering from mental illness, but unfortunately, most of those suffering in that way know something's just not right. Living with someone who has a mental illness can be a real challenge. The following is only two of the challenges I faced with my mother.

I don't think my mother knew she had a mental illness, but we all certainly felt its effects. She knew she was miserable all the time, and she used all kinds of medicines to try to remedy how she felt. When one didn't do the job, she'd mix in another. In addition to self-medicating that way, she began drinking. That was a dangerous combination that could easily have been lethal. It didn't kill her then, but it made for adventurous times.

Most teenagers get their driving experience under the supervision of their parents on multiple trips to a variety of destinations. I got one driving lesson from my mom, just one, and it was a doozy. After our family car was repossessed, Mom had to buy an old beater, a dented, tan, '70s Chrysler LeBaron. I'd had my permit for several months but hadn't done any driving. At that time, my mom was either at work or asleep, and I wasn't home much either. I went to school and worked twenty to thirty hours a week, mostly in restaurants. I spent what little free time I had with friends and boyfriends.

But my mom and I were home one particular evening when she asked if I wanted to learn to drive. Of course I did! It was late, and it was dark; that made me nervous, but I had to take what I could get. I'd never been behind the wheel, and there I was getting my first driving lesson. In the dark. That was two strikes against me. Mom changed her clothes and grabbed her purse. We climbed into the car.

We had been driving for about half an hour when I turned onto a two-lane road in a residential area. Parked cars lined both sides of the road. As I was cresting a small knoll, my mom snatched the steering wheel and yanked it. We crashed into a parked car. It was surreal. "What the heck just happened?" I asked. "Why did you do that?"

"I thought you were crossing over the middle," she said. But I hadn't crossed over. *Why would she think that?* We climbed out of the car to survey the damage. I was standing with my mom by the wrecked car when a police car pulled up. Only a few minutes had passed—not enough time for anyone to have called the police. My mom asked me, "Can you smell anything on my breath?" At that moment, I realized Mom had been drinking.

The officer spoke to us and lectured my mom about not touching the steering wheel. "Just verbally guide the driver." The officer found the car's owner and brought him outside. We exchanged information. It was later that my mom told me she didn't have any insurance and neither did the victim of our crash. Mom negotiated with the other party, and they agreed on a payment of $300. Turns out, I had to pay for the damages. At $3.35 per hour—minimum wage at that time—it took me almost six weeks to pay that off.

I was angry at my mom for a long time. She was my mom, the adult who was supposed to guide me and help direct my life, but instead, she was reckless and had made me pay for her irresponsible behavior. We didn't have a good relationship to start with, but that was the beginning of a rift that never closed between us. And the good times kept on rollin'.

My sense of humor is not always of the happy, light-hearted type. Lots of sarcasm and satire float around my home. At a time when we're supposed to be politically correct, my family always speaks to each other with brutal honesty. The joke in our house is that I come from a long line of crazy Asian women so don't mess with me.

I dropped out of high school four months before I was to graduate. I did really well until my senior year, but then I started dating older guys, staying out until the wee hours of the morning, working, and skipping school. I was rarely home. When I was, my mom was usually medicated.

One Friday night when I was seventeen, I came home with my boyfriend, Jack. I was going to spend the weekend at his place, so we stopped by my family's apartment to pick up some clothes. My brother Jimmy was sitting on the couch. My mom had been drinking. She asked what I was doing. I told her I was going to spend the weekend with Jack. Her response was, "Over my dead body!"

I ignored her. I headed to my bedroom to pack a bag. Jack stayed and waited for me in the living room. When I came out of my room, my mom grabbed my arm. We began to argue. *Really? Is she going to begin parenting me now?* I'd been on my own for too many of my adolescent years. Since I was independent and self-sufficient, I wasn't about to let her tell me what to do. *She hasn't participated in my life the past few years, so why should I listen to her now?* That was the attitude of my hardened heart. I'd walked away from God four years prior to that and had been swallowed by the world and all it had to offer.

I ripped my arm away from Mom's grasp. Jack and I headed for the door. She ran into the kitchen, grabbed a large meat knife, and charged at me with it. I ran around the furniture in the living room, into the dining room, and around the dining room table. She chased me around the table several times and somehow cornered me. When I thought I had no chance of escape, I turned and tucked my head into the corner and gave up. I couldn't watch my own death.

There's fear and then there's fear. To this day, I've not felt anything like the terror I felt that day. I'll never forget what that felt like. As I stood there with my head pressed up against the corner, I clenched my fists to my cheeks, closed my eyes tight, and waited for the inevitable.

I felt something dragging down the back of my tweed

coat. I thought that being stabbed with a knife would have been more painful. I turned and saw that Jack and my brother Jimmy had wrestled Mom to the ground. Jack pried the knife out of her hand and threw it out the back door into the woods. We all ran out the front door. That dragging feeling had been the knife running down the back of my coat when Jack and Jimmy grabbed her just as she lunged at my back.

We called the police. They arrived, took our statements, and talked to my mom. The police told us we could have her committed to an institution but we would have to go to court the following morning, file papers, and work our way through the judicial system. They told me that since I was seventeen, I'd be placed in a foster home until the next month, when I would turn eighteen.

The officer had pity on me. He took me aside and said that having my mother committed would accomplish nothing. He said that it would be better for me to find a place to live for the next few weeks, until my birthday. I would then legally be an adult, and she couldn't touch me.

I sent Jimmy into the house for my clothes and left with what little I owned—a few bags of clothes. I stayed at Jack's place for a couple of weeks, and then we moved to his parents' home in Pennsylvania.

Just before I turned eighteen, my mother called the authorities and had a warrant issued for my arrest. I still don't understand what she was trying to accomplish; maybe she wanted me back home? The warrant indicated that I was a "minor in need of counseling." A runaway or juvenile delinquent maybe?

I went back to Virginia and showed up in a juvenile counselor's office to answer the charges. When I told her the whole story and the background of neglect leading to my leaving, she said, "I think *she* should be arrested instead of you." She said I could be dismissed. She said she would advise my mother to drop the matter or she would press charges of child neglect on my mother. I cried throughout the conversation with that counselor. She was so kind and compassionate. I remember only a handful of times in my childhood that I felt an adult cared about me, and that was one of them.

It seemed all so natural and normal. I'd been working since I was thirteen and taking care of myself, so my move wasn't a difficult adjustment. I lived with Jack and his parents while I took my GED course and passed the test. I received my certificate before my class graduated in June that year.

For years, I've had dreams in which I go back to high school and take classes to get my diploma, but in my dreams, I'm always my current age—twenty-six, thirty-five, forty-one … I didn't think graduating from high school was important back then, but on some level, it obviously still bothers me.

CHAPTER NINE

CONTROL

You must learn to let go.
You were never in control anyway.
—Steve Maraboli, author of *Life, the Truth, and Being Free*

This is by far the most difficult part of my life to write about. However, since it's such an integral part of my life and was influential in forming my character, I have to relate it.

He would come into my bedroom in the dark. Because I didn't know what to do, I pretended I was asleep. I was afraid. Of what? I had no idea, but when you're six, everything's scary.

It happened quite often until I was thirteen. We had moved over three thousand miles from home and had started a new life. When I was thirteen, I finally found the courage to stop it. I was filled with anger and no longer willing to pretend to be asleep.

After I stopped the abuse, I became even angrier, but that anger was focused inward, at myself. I was angry I hadn't stopped it sooner. I blamed myself for being the victim for so long. Everything I did after that was classic, textbook behavior for anyone who experiences sexual abuse. This chronic abuse left me with many issues that threw wrenches into my life. I had inexplicable bouts of rage and a constant need to control everything; I was obsessive-compulsive. I became rebellious and promiscuous. It was as if I had jumped out of the frying pan and straight into the fire. To this day, I become enraged when I hear or read about any child being sexually abused. My heart breaks for them

The sexual abuse I suffered has affected every aspect of my life. Relationships were always a struggle for me. I stuffed the abuse away and didn't think about it or deal with it. When I was in my thirties, I had an emotional meltdown after a manic bipolar episode. For the sake of my husband and children, I had to seek help.

With the support and love of my husband, Matthew, I sought counseling. Through the counseling, I figured out that the abuse I had experienced as a child made me feel I had no control over my life, so when anyone tried to control me verbally or physically, it would set me off. I'd fight back, unlike when I was a child and couldn't. I was determined that no one was going to control me.

A combination of therapy and medicine helped me

sort out my emotions so I could manage these issues when they popped up in daily life. I hung onto the anger and resentment I had for him. I fed off it, and it gave me the illusion of power and strength. You wanna talk about hell on earth? Just experience unforgiveness toward someone. Then, one day, I heard, "Not forgiving is like drinking poison and waiting for the other person to die." It made me wonder if I was poisoning myself with hatred. That led to much self-examination.

I was trying to grow in my Christian faith, but I felt I'd hit a wall. The anger and hate was like a concrete block charm on my necklace. I knew that if I was going to grow spiritually, I had to let it go and somehow forgive him. But how? I didn't know where to begin, so I did what I knew. I prayed. I pleaded desperately, "Lord, I don't know how to forgive him. Please show me how!" And in time, he did.

He made me see myself as I really was—a sinner saved by his grace and mercy. Matthew 18: 23–35 tells the parable of a master and his servant who owed his master a debt. When the servant couldn't repay it, the master ordered that all the servant's possessions, including his wife and children, be sold to repay the debt. The servant fell to his knees and begged the master for mercy. The master had mercy on him and forgave the debt. However, when that same servant went to a second servant to collect a debt, the second servant couldn't pay it back. He also begged for mercy, but the first servant had the second servant thrown in jail. When the servant's master heard this, he became angry and had him put in jail.

I saw myself as the servant. My Master had forgiven all my sins through the sacrifice of his Son, Jesus Christ, but I hadn't forgiven this man of his sin against me. You could say that my sins weren't as evil as the sin my abuser had committed upon me, but a sin is a sin plain and simple; in God's eyes, there isn't a measurement for sin. When God forgives our sins, he forgives them all, no matter how we humans measure them. And there isn't a single sin God won't forgive. He knows our hearts, and therein lies forgiveness.

I've truly forgiven my offender and repaired our relationship. I cannot describe the feeling of freedom I experienced other than as a pure joy and weightlessness.

I have compassion for those who have experienced the same as I have but are outraged by my forgiveness. Many of those who have been abused feel justified in holding onto hate for the perpetrators. Yes, it's their right to do so, but I've found that life is a blink of an eye. One minute you're sixteen, and the next, you're forty. Life is short, and it is hard. Why wear that concrete block around your neck when you can live with the amazing joy that comes from the freedom of forgiveness?

I think about what happened to me in the same way Joseph did after his brothers sold him into slavery: "You intended to harm me, but God intended it for good to accomplish what is now being done" (Genesis 50:20 NIV).

CHAPTER TEN

SAY IT NOW

Do it now. Sometimes, "later" becomes "never."
—Anonymous

God wants each of us to come to him. He wants to have a re-lationship with us so we can know him. Some are introduced to him at church camp, some through ministries that help families, and some through neighbors, friends, and family members. The universal theme is that God uses *people* to bring the unsaved to him.

I was twenty-two and a train wreck. One bad decision after another (including an abusive first marriage) had had a snowball effect. My life up to that point had been the same drama repeated over and over. I spent my days constantly putting out fires. As soon as I put one out, another would blaze up. It was emotionally exhausting. Had it not been for the love of a good man, I'd still be living that life.

The man God chose for me wasn't a perfect man, but he knew God. He was a flawed man, a sinner just like me. I hate to say it because it's so corny but Matthew was an officer and a gentlemen. He was a non-commissioned officer in the U S Army. I was working two jobs. I was an insurance agent during the day and I waited tables at a small restaurant in Arlington, Virginia. Matthew was stationed at the Pentagon, and he came with friends to have dinner. While making small talk, we discovered we lived in the same building across the street from the restaurant. We struck up a friendship. I'd never known kindness and love like his. He cared more about me than himself; he didn't insult me, curse me, or threaten me with any kind of violence. He was gentle and loving, unlike any man I'd ever known. I had no examples of what a good man was, but I knew he made me feel safe. God had sent me a protector. I realized that if I wanted to change my life, I couldn't continue doing the same things over and over and expecting different results. I made the decision to follow this man from Washington, DC, to his home in Pennsylvania.

One year later, I married him. Matthew, my knight in shining armor, became my husband. To this day, we tease Matthew by calling him "Prince Matthew." With him, I learned what love and family were meant to be. His wasn't a perfect family, but it was filled with people who loved one another. My mother-in-law, Marian, is the kindest and most gentle person I know. She's not a perfect woman, but she loves God. (You notice a theme here? Not a perfect man, not a perfect family, not a perfect woman? I'll get back to this later.)

The fact that my mother-in-law remained godly after raising four rambunctious boys speaks of the great depth of her faith. When asked if she felt she'd lived an extraordinary life for Christ, she said no. She had lived her ordinary life and had raised her sons to know God. Nothing extraordinary. But it was her son's love and encouragement that brought a lost, hopeless young woman back to God.

You parents out there raising your children in the knowledge of the Lord, don't ever underestimate the power of an "unextraordinary," God-centered life.

Marian was also my example of what a mother was supposed to be. I thank God for placing her in my life; without her, how could I have been a mother of four and more? I had had no positive motherly influences in my life—not one.

I learned from her about self-sacrifice and kindness, but most important, I learned that her faith was what sustained her through all her trials. So I followed suit. If you knew me, you'd ask me how I could do what I have to do every day—raising four children, caring for my household, working, and running a youth ranch. Crazy doesn't even begin to cover it. But God gives me the strength I need for each day. No matter how bad the previous day was or how bad I was, God's mercy and grace is new every day.

Remember what I said earlier about not a perfect man, not a perfect family, not a perfect woman? God doesn't expect us to be perfect or even good enough to have a relationship with him. He loves us just as we are, imperfect. He does amazing things every day using imperfect people. People like you and me. So whether you're "just" a housewife or a veritable "Billy Graham," the ripple effects of your everyday life go further than you can imagine.

While I was in Pennsylvania, I received a call from my mom. I hadn't spoken to her since the night she'd tried to kill me. She had gotten my number from my sister. When we spoke, she apologized for what she had done, and she asked how I was. It had been five years. After I hung up, I thought that perhaps we could begin to mend our relationship. Just a few weeks later, she committed suicide.

I don't know why I was so surprised that she had taken her life; I don't remember my mom ever being happy. For most of her life, she was tormented by such a deep depression that I should have expected it, and yet I was shocked.

This woman had been to hell and back, so to speak. She had managed to keep six children alive in the worst of circumstances. She'd survived hunger, beatings, homelessness, and war. She was tough. *Why did she give up now?* I was overwhelmed by the thought that there would be no mending of our relationship. It was too late. My mother was dead at age fifty-two. She wouldn't attend my wedding to Matthew or be there when I gave birth to my first child.

Good or bad, I learned to say it *now* and not expect there to be a *later*. When you realize there are no guarantees you'll have a tomorrow, you have to ask yourself, *What happens if I die today?* This is why I feel such an urgency to reach out to children who don't know about Jesus Christ. With every generation, God is fading.

I flew to California for my mother's funeral. It was the last time my siblings and I were all together. Why was it that only death could bring all six of us together? True to her crazy nature, Letty brought balloons and a cake to the funeral service. She wanted to celebrate Mom's life rather than mourn her death.

Death comes swiftly, but what comes before and after is such a long, drawn-out process. After receiving the news, you have to make funeral arrangements, then the viewing, then the funeral, and finally, you have to deal with the deceased's possessions. We had to clean out her apartment. My siblings and I each chose a room and went to work. I stood in her bedroom and stared at the bed where her life had left her. I felt an incredible depth of sorrow as I considered how hopeless she must have felt to have taken her life. Words cannot adequately describe that pain.

I began packing up her belongings, starting on my knees beside a pile of scattered papers. My intention was to gather them and put them in the bag. I'm not usually one for details, but my eyes were drawn to one particular letter. The letterhead read, "Private Investigator." *That's weird. Why would Mom hire a PI?* I skimmed the information. "James Standlee ... resides in Orlando, Florida ... I can assure you without a doubt that this is the James Standlee you are looking for."

Whoa! In my hand was contact information for the father I'd never known. That was before the Internet, before you could find someone with a few clicks of a mouse. When I was little, my mother had mentioned that he had remarried, but she didn't talk about him much. I was only twenty-three at the time, but I had experienced enough of life to know there were two sides to every story. I knew what little my mom had told me; I wanted to hear his side.

I had a phone number for my father, but I just couldn't bring myself to call him. I was afraid he would reject me. So after going home and settling in, I wrote to my father.

I thought you should know that my mother, your first wife,
has died. I grew up with a certain image of you based
on what my mother told me. I'm older now, and I know
things are not always what they appear to be.
I would like to hear your side of the story.

Ample time went by without a reply. Unbeknownst to me, my husband-to-be, Matthew, called my father. My father had snapped at him, "It's none of your damn business!" and hung up.

I mentioned to my sister that I had written to James but hadn't received a response. She matter of factly pronounced in her Vietnamese accent, "Oh! I call him. Give me his number. He talk to me." A few days later, I heard my dad's voice for the first time. It took Letty days of praying for God to take away the anger that she had for my father and the years of abuse. She had to get past that so she could contact him on my behalf. Letty knew that I needed to know him so that I could have closure now that my mom was gone.

We spoke frequently, and Matthew and I later flew to Orlando to meet him. That gap in my life slowly closed. Forgiveness was a must for a new start. We kept in touch for the next eighteen years, but there was never that closeness for which I had longed. Over the years, I learned many things about my father. Knowing his history of drinking and physical abuse and his unapologetic, racist beliefs made it abundantly clear to me why God hadn't allowed my father to be a part of my life.

All my life I had wanted a father present in my life, but I finally understood why I couldn't have one. As bad as my childhood was, I'm sure it would have been worse with him. Instead of learning compassion, I might have learned hate.

I can speak to those of you whose fathers abandoned you and assure you that it was God's plan, and God doesn't make mistakes. Trust him. It may not make sense now, but if you seek him, he will help you understand. I can also speak to you Christan men. Be a positive male role model to just one child outside of your immediate family. Just one. You may never know how far reaching your efforts will be on behalf of Jesus Christ.

My father received the gifts my mother should have received. He was there when I celebrated my wedding to Matthew. He was given four grandchildren. He became their grandfather and enjoyed all the privileges that came with it—and then he dropped out of our lives without notice.

My father and I no longer speak, but that's okay. When he chose to abandon me for the second time, I didn't feel the emptiness I had felt when I was a child. I realized I had had my Father with me all my life. He never left me; I just chose not to see him. My Father was there for every tear of hopelessness and every laughter of happiness.

Be strong and courageous. Do not be afraid ...
for the Lord your God goes with you;
he will never leave you or forsake you.
—Deuteronomy 31:6 NIV

CHAPTER ELEVEN
THE CENTURION

Give to everyone what you owe them: If you owe taxes,
pay taxes; if revenue, then revenue;
if respect, then respect; if honor, then honor.
—Romans 13:7 NIV

One of my favorite sayings hangs on my kitchen wall.

One hundred years from now,
it will not matter how much money you had,
the sort of house you lived in,
or the kind of car you drove,
but the world is a better place
because you made a difference in the life of a child.

As I traveled the three-and-a-half-hours to Gettys-burg, Pennsylvania, I spent much of the time contemplating what it would be like to live a hundred years. I imagined what I would have seen and experienced over ten decades, especially those spanning the twentieth century.

The first commercial airplane flight took place in 1914, and World War I raged on from that year through 1918. During the 1920s, automobiles were mass produced for the first time and progress was made in the development of the television. The Great Depression hit America in 1929. The photocopier was invented in 1939, and a computer with software was developed in 1941. That same year, World War II erupted, ending in 1945 with the first use of atomic bombs.

Microwave ovens were invented in 1946, and the earliest mobile phone system was rolled out in 1946. The civil rights movement brought great changes between 1954 and 1968, and America's involvement in the Vietnam War lasted from 1954 to 1975. By the mid-1990s, the Internet was in widespread use.

These inventions and events have had such profound effects on the world. I was surprised to discover when some of these items were created. A computer in 1941? A photocopier in 1937? Really? Life has changed so drastically so quickly. A horse-and-wagon trip that took days now takes only hours in a car. Illnesses and infections that caused so many deaths now require only a few pills to conquer. Appliances have helped us drastically cut the time we spend on housework.

It's only when we look back and study life in the past that we have a full appreciation (or not) of what modern life offers us. Some think the endless communication options we have today are wonderful and helpful, while many others point to the distractions they present. In any case, a hundred years is a long time to live.

I was blessed to share in a hundredth birthday celebration for Reuben Johnson near Gettysburg, Pennsylvania. Mr. Johnson was the church deacon who had volunteered to sign the papers that made him fully responsible for my family so we could come to the United States. He had purchased a home for us to live in out of the sheer kindness of his heart.

The only thing I remembered about Mr. Johnson was that every Christmas, he would bring us a box of apples. As I became more accustomed to American Christmas traditions, my attitude turned sour. I was disappointed when he brought us just apples; what I really wanted was presents. I see now that he was bringing us the sustenance we so desperately needed. I remember being hungry often, especially at the end of the month before the food stamps came again.

I hadn't seen Mr. Johnson since I was eleven. Presented with the opportunity to see him again, I wanted very much to express my gratitude. The closer I got to Gettysburg, the deeper that yearning became. I needed him to know that the sacrifices he had made had not been for nothing. "So is my word that goes out from my mouth: It will not return to me empty, but will accomplish what I desire and achieve the purpose for which I sent it" (Isaiah 55:11 NIV). What he did was a part of bringing one of God's lost sheep back into the fold—and this redeemed sheep is now living for him.

Mr. Johnson was almost sixty when he signed for my family and bought that house. At a time when most people are looking toward retirement and slowing down, he made a huge personal and financial commitment. In a world in which many fathers abandon their children, what kind of a man takes on the burden of a whole other family? Surely, he was a man who loved the Lord. People do things for those they know and love, sure, but why do some people do things for people they've never met? He never put any conditions on us or pressed us for anything in return. Maybe it's just me, but I don't see much of that type of sacrificial love in our world today. I know those kinds of people exist; I read and hear about them, but they seem so rare.

Matthew and I arrived at our hotel the evening prior to the party. We had settled in and were awaiting the arrival of my sister and her husband, Henry. We'd agreed to share a room. What we got was entertainment for the evening.

We were staying just one night, but Letty rolled in with a luggage cart. She and Henry each had a travel bag, but the boxes of food she had brought had me laughing. She lived in an area where there were many good Vietnamese restaurants, and true to her loving nature, Letty was sweet enough to buy some Vietnamese food as a gift for Matthew and me.

Our peaceful room quickly became host to the Tasmanian devil as my sister whirled around the room. I looked at Henry quizzically. He laughed and said not to worry, that she rearranged all the furniture every time they went to a hotel. She moved chairs, luggage, the desk, clothing—everything. When she finally finished making us a "dining" area, she began to unwrap the food, enough to feed a small village.

We had a nice hotel room with a refrigerator and microwave, but I couldn't heat the food in the Styrofoam containers as they would melt. Letty's response in her Vietnamese accent was, "No problem, I find sometin." She dug into her bag and proclaimed, "Here you go!"

I burst out laughing. "Who does that? Who just whips Tupperware out of their purse?"

"I live tru da war. I make anyting work," she announced.

Henry rolled his eyes. "Nine hours in the car with her, I need a beer."

We were all laughing and didn't stop laughing for two hours. We needed napkins. She extracted a five-inch pile of them from a bag. We needed spoons. She plopped down fifteen or so plastic spoons. When the bag was empty, she tied it around the lamp by the headboard so we'd have an extra trash can. I raised my eyebrows but didn't say anything. I was thinking, *This one, she's a character.*

Letty's always been different. She packed fifteen washcloths for one night's stay because "Da hotel neva give you enough washclots." Apparently, she bathed three or four times a day.

She yelled out of the bathroom, "Henry, go get more toilet paper."

"But there's a roll and a half, and we're only gonna be here one night," he said. He tried to argue with her, but he put his shoes on.

"Why are you getting more toilet paper?" I asked.

Henry's exasperated but comical response was, "Because she won't stop until I do."

Matt burst out laughing. Henry came back with two rolls that of course we didn't use.

Because there were times when we had nothing, my sister had become a surplus queen. When she buys anything, it's always in excess. She'll buy ten or fifteen tubes of toothpaste at a time. I've seen supplies oozing out of the cabinets at her home. It's a side effect of life during war; similar to those who lived through the Great Depression don't waste or throw anything away.

As we were eating the delicious food, Henry proceeded to tell us "Letty stories" since we hadn't seen each other in some time. My sister is very talented with art and flower arranging. She'd made a silk flower arrangement for my mother's grave in Virginia as well as for Henry's mom's grave in New Jersey.

When she mentioned to a friend that she was doing this, her friend asked her to place flowers on her grandmother's grave in the same cemetery as my mom's grave. Being the kind person she is, my sister said yes. On Thanksgiving Day, Henry and Letty arrived at the cemetery. She put the flowers on my mother's grave, and then they looked for her friend's grandmother's grave. Henry asked, "What's the name we're looking for?"

"Something Nguyen," Letty answered. Nguyen, the most common Vietnamese name, is used in probably 70 percent of Vietnamese names, and there were many Vietnamese in our area of Virginia. They spent two hours walking around a dark cemetery in the freezing rain hoping they didn't get locked in. They never did find the grave site. Reason #1001 why we call her Crazy Aunt Letty. Sometimes, it's a hare-brained idea, and other times, it's her kindness, but she always seems to get herself into a pickle.

Henry told us that just for once, on this Thanksgiving, all he wanted was a nice turkey dinner, but Letty insisted they go to an all-you-can-eat seafood buffet. Letty always gets her way. When they finally got to bed, Letty didn't sleep long. She woke up in the middle of the night and couldn't go back to sleep, so she decided to go Black Friday shopping.

Henry woke up and discovered Letty was gone. He called her cell phone. She assured him she was fine and told him to go back to bed.

Henry called her every hour to make sure she was okay—2:00 a.m., 3:00 a.m., 4:00 a.m. Henry told us, "We didn't get to New Jersey until almost dark because of Letty's Black Friday antics."

Insulted by that comment, Letty stated matter of fact-ly, "Da sun set earlier in New York dan it does in DC, so we get dere close to dak [dark]."

"What? How's that possible? New York and DC are in the same time zone."

Henry said they had gotten off to a late start because crazy Letty had been busy Black Friday shopping and was running on only two hours of sleep. And of course she had to drive because she always wants to be in control.

Arriving at the cemetery in New Jersey, they found all the gates were closed and locked but one. While Henry tried to find his mother's grave, Letty, in the driver's seat, made sure the car was facing the gate so she could ram it if they got locked in. I say that seriously. I know it sounds crazy, but this is my sister we're talking about.

She said, "No way I get stuck in creepy cemetery wit' old headstone and iron gates." Henry said it was worse than Ricky Ricardo living with Lucy. All the mischief Lucille Ball got into on *I Love Lucy* doesn't even begin to touch the predicaments Letty gets into. It has to be exhausting being Henry.

Henry went on with another story. They had flown to Greece for vacation; since Henry worked for the airline, they flew on standby. If a flight was full, they would have to wait for the next flight. It took them forty-eight hours to get to Greece. Once my sister arrived, she crashed. She was still sleeping when Henry went to check out the hotel. Apparently, the door locked when Henry left, and my sister couldn't get out. She decided to step out on the balcony to see if she could get some help. Fortunately for her, the young couple staying in the next room was on their balcony and were able to contact the front desk to unlock Letty's door.

Later that day, my sister noticed that the couple had a rental car. My sister can do anything on a budget, especially traveling. With this new discovery, she realized they could save money if she and Henry tagged along with the couple, so she devised a plan to see them.

The next morning, Henry and Letty got up early and packed for the day. They listened for any noise from next door. A short while later, they heard a chair drag across the floor, so Letty dressed quickly and tried to find an unopened gift to give the neighbors. There was a box of bread, but it was open. She had a pile of snacks, but they had been opened also. Letty had purchased some guava juice when they arrived in Greece the previous day. She grabbed the bottle. Juice in hand, she knocked on the unsuspecting couple's door. In her best, over-the-top, friendly manner, she told them, "Tank you so much fo' heping me yeterday. Dis is a gif' fo' you."

She made small talk before going in for the kill. "Oh, I see you going somewhere."

"Yes, we're going to the beach."

Letty said, "Oh! If we pay for the gas, can we come along?"

Really? Who invites themselves? Especially with people they barely know? To my astonishment, the couple said yes.

My sister is not a mooch; on her behalf, I'll say she paid for the couple's beach chairs and lunch. Later, the couple invited Henry and Letty to dinner. My sister has a very outgoing personality, as you can tell, so it was no surprise when the couple invited Henry and Letty along for most of their activities that week, and everyone had fun. They even affectionately named her "The American Nightmare." Reason #1002 why we call her Crazy Aunty Nuet.

The next day, we drove to New Oxford, Pennsylvania, for the birthday celebration. Once we had checked in and received our name badges, we found a table. I looked around and realized my chair was behind a pillar that blocked my view of the small stage where Mr. Johnson was sitting. When I peeked around the pillar, I saw his familiar, round face. Yes, he had aged, but not so much that he was unrecognizable. His skin was pale, not tanned as I remembered. His hair was already white when I met him in 1975, so that hadn't changed—he just had less of it. My sister and I made our way to him.

I was concerned he wouldn't be mentally sharp. Letty

said, "Hello, Mr. Johnson. Happy birthday! This is my sister Micheline. Do you remember her?"

Without hesitation, he responded, "Why yes. You were the youngest one. Living in Pennsylvania." He had remembered what my sister had mentioned to him months earlier. I introduced him to my husband. We didn't share many words, but I recalled that Mr. Johnson was never a big talker. Others at the party confirmed he was quick to listen but slow to speak; he wasn't a man for frivolous words; he said it straight, plain, and simple.

Tears welled up in my eyes. "I wanted to thank you for what you did for me and my family. I know what a sacrifice it was, and I appreciate it so much."

He nodded and smiled. "You're welcome."

What I learned about him that day amazed me. I knew he had a daughter, but apparently, he had seven children! Five were birth children. A son had died before he was one. They had adopted two boys, who attended his church.

When the mother ran off with another man who became an alcoholic, Mr. Johnson and his wife took in and raised the nine- and fourteen-year-olds. I learned that he had been a civil engineer who had traveled the world for his work. He was given a deferment from World War II, but as the war dragged on, he felt he needed to help, so he joined the navy in 1944.

From the day he became saved, when he was six, Rueben was a godly man in word and action. He was such an influence on his children that three are now serving the Lord either as pastors or in ministries. He also was instrumental in planting several new churches. In the 1970s, he and his wife, Bernice, smuggled bibles into Communist countries. I heard testimonials from many about the tender, loving care he gave to his wife of over sixty-eight years when she became ill.

He had such a busy, full life with traveling and a large family, but as my sister said, "A man with a big family [six kids and grandchildren] barely has time for his own, but to commit to and care for my large family in addition?" He didn't do this completely on his own, but that doesn't negate the power of his quiet influence on my life.

I also discovered what a humble man he was. When showered with compliments by the many speakers on that day, his response was, "Compliments are like perfume; you want to smell it but you don't want to drink it."

When she came to America, Letty came under "refugee" status. She told me that when she was in her early twenties, she tried to obtain a permanent U.S. resident card but was denied time after time. Among the many reasons, the State Department said it couldn't grant her permanent residency because it couldn't confirm whether my mother had taken her illegally from her father. She was so frustrated and had no idea what to do. She mentioned it to Mr. Johnson. He said, "We're gonna take care of this." And he did. He fought the State Department with such intelligent arguments that it could no longer deny her.

Mr. Johnson had a long life of loving and helping so many people. That was made obvious by the numerous people in attendance at the party. Because of that, I wasn't able to hold a long conversation or ask him many questions, but I thanked and hugged him again as we said our good-byes.

As a part of my spiritual growth, I've realized that God reveals on a "need to know" basis. Mr. Johnson simply did what God told him to do; he didn't attach strings or make demands. He and his church just loved us in action with the hope that one day, we would see our need for salvation and walk with Christ.

I'm results-oriented. If I do something but don't see instant results, I get frustrated and take it personally. With all the work involved in starting up our youth ranch and mentoring program (I'll get into this in the next chapter), I fear

I won't be able to help the children who will come. I worry I won't know what to say or do. I have no training in psychology or child behavior; I just know I have a gift that many don't—I love others; showing kindness comes easily for me.

Rueben Johnson helped me see that I need to keep doing what God commands and let him bring about the positive results. I may not see the results right away—they may be down the road—but I know that's not where my focus should be; it has to be on loving each child in word and deed here and now. I have to trust that the Lord will provide the words I need to say to each broken heart and that he will reveal the actions I need to take. Mr. Johnson's favorite Bible verse is so befitting.

Trust in the Lord with all your heart and lean not
on your own understanding; in all your ways
submit to him, and he will make your paths straight.
—Proverbs 3:5–6 NIV

Three months later, in February 2015, Mr. Johnson passed away. I thank God for the opportunity to have seen him again and extend my gratitude to him before he went to be with the Lord.

CHAPTER TWELVE
AHA!

We go through the present blindfolded ...
Only later, when the blindfold is removed and
we examine the past, do we realize what we've
been through and understand what it means.
—Milan Kundera

We humans are curious; we have a need for understanding. Most of us have experienced that moment when true understanding finally soaks in. You know, when that lightbulb comes on. It could be the punch line to a joke that didn't register for a minute or so. For me, it was like being pregnant and knowing something big was growing in me spiritually, but in no way could I describe it. The journey also took nine months from the beginning "Why am I here?" to the "Wow! It all makes sense now!"

In the fall of 2009, I was selling real estate and met a new client. Tom was a fellow believer. During our first conversation, he asked me, "What are you passionate about?" I had never been asked that before. I had to think about it, but my gut didn't take long to respond. Kids. It was why my husband and I decided to become foster parents four years earlier. When the church we were attending fell apart, we came together with some of the other former members and became founding members of a fledgling church. That began the spiritual revival in our family.

Anytime you seek God, it changes you. I don't care how old you are or where you live, he opens your eyes and really changes you. I'd spent my whole life working harder and anticipating more money so we could have more things; I figured that I'd be happy then. Matthew and I took stock of our lives and saw how blessed we were, particularly given my background. We had employment, four healthy children, and a roof over our heads.

Once you become a believer in Jesus Christ and truly love the Lord, you'll have a deep desire to serve him, and he will burden your heart for someone. It could be for the home- less, the elderly, abused children, veterans, or many others.

Most of us are so busy with our lives that we ignore that burden, that little tap on our shoulders. We won't even feel that burden if our spiritual life is nonexistent. I had such a burden to help children, and I knew it was because of the adversities I had experienced as a child. But it wasn't until I was forty-one that I realized the adversities weren't only my driving factor but also had prepared me to help the children to come.

So many hurting people don't think that others can identify with them unless they've experienced the same hurt. We experience bad things in this world because sin exists. But God uses the bad and turns it into good. So the choice lies with us. Do we want to be bitter or better from our experiences? Life is very short, and I can tell you being bitter is miserable.

My husband and I quickly realized that the fostering system was broken. We were told to parent our foster children the same way we would our own, but then they took away our authority as parents. Perfect example: we had a foster child who wanted to attend a gay and lesbian conference. That wasn't an activity we would have allowed our children to participate in; it was against our moral beliefs. However, when we said no, the child called her caseworker and asked to be removed from the home.

We've had other foster children who just didn't like the rules we had in place, so they would simply place a call and would be moved. We wanted to find another way to reach out to broken children and show them the love of God.

My client Tom, who posed the question about my passion, told me to check out Crystal Peaks Youth Ranch in Bend, Oregon. CPYR was a faith-based nonprofit that rescued horses and teamed up a horse, a volunteer mentor, and a child in need.

At that time, CPYR had been running its mentoring program successfully for almost fifteen years. Kim, a cofounder of CPYR, had lost her mom and dad in a murder-suicide situation when she was young. When she went to live with her grandmother, her grandmother got her a horse that God used to save her life.

Because of their obedience to God, Kim and cofounder Troy Meeder have been blessed beyond measure, and they wanted others to do the same. They started offering annual information clinics so others could start their own ranches.

My husband and I attended a CPYR information clinic in May 2010. We learned so much there, but the one thing I'll never forget was Troy Meeder saying, "If you make the commitment to do a ranch, the minute you head down our driveway, Satan *will* attack."

Troy was right. Satan got busy using our family, chil-

dren, neighbors and our local township government to dis-
courage us. It was when I got home from the information
clinic that I had my *Aha!* moment. It all made sense. Why else
would he pair up a broken, little, half-Vietnamese girl with a
Christian man who had been raised on a farm with horses and
then bless them with lots of land? Without my husband's farm
experience, we wouldn't have survived the five years since we
started the ranch. His farming knowledge and skills were ex-
actly what we needed. Without what I had experienced, how
could I have compassion to help these kids?

Our goal for our ranch is to bring together a rescue
horse, a child in need, and a volunteer mentor. Each time a
child visits, the mentor and child do a thirty-minute chore
together such as cleaning out a stall or painting a gate. Sixty
minutes will go into teaching the child how to ride.

The kids who don't want to ride will have other activity options, but they will still be offered the security and love
of a caring mentor all free of charge. Our typical child is an
average kid, six to eighteen years old, who is dealing with
everyday life issues such as divorce, bullying, death, abuse,
and family problems.

Five months later, we incorporated as Ready Yourselves Youth Ranch. We chose our ranch name from a Casting

Crowns song, "Until the Whole World Hears." Matthew and I had been racking our brains for a ranch name, and while he was driving in his car, he heard the lyrics of the song, and God laid it on his heart.

> *Wanna be your hands and feet,*
> *Wanna live a life that leads.*
> *Ready yourselves, ready yourselves.*
> *Let us shine the light of Jesus in the darkest night.*

The lyrics strongly encompassed what we wanted to do. We *do* want to be his servants, we *do* want to live so we can be beacons to draw others to Jesus. We *are* getting ready for his coming. So many children are living in the darkest nights of their lives right now, and we want so much to be the light of Jesus.

Another piece of advice from Troy and Kim Meeder was to be as "transparent" as we could be. With that in mind, I discussed what we wanted to do with our local code enforcement officer Barry. He verified, based on our agricultural zoning, that having this ranch on our twenty acres was acceptable. Our joy was quickly dashed when we shared the news of our venture with our neighbors, thinking they would be supportive. Boy, were we wrong.

We later learned that several of the neighbors had protested to the township authorities, which spurred Barry to call us in for a second meeting. He told us we'd be required to obtain a permit to operate our ranch. Little did we know the havoc that was about to be unleashed.

While we took steps to obtain our permit, the word went out about our ranch, and we received so many calls about horses in need. We cleared some of the wooded area at the back of our property to prepare paddocks, fenced-in holding areas for our horses. Because the paddock was so far away from our house, we had no access to electricity or water. The township wouldn't allow us to build a barn, so we erected temporary shelters. One of my goals was to learn about horses; I knew absolutely nothing about them.

Those who know horses are saying to themselves right now, *Wow. This lady was crazy!* She started a ranch and knew nothing about horses! I learned that horses are hard enough to care for with a barn, water, and electricity, but we had none of those things. Horses eat money, and they poop work. A lot of money. And a lot of work. I had no idea how much work they were, how much they cost, and how physically challenging and emotionally complicated each horse could be due to its history, especially rescue horses.

But the Lord had asked us to step out of the boat in complete, blind faith. We trusted that if this was what God wanted us to do, he would open the doors and show us the way. That didn't mean, however, the path would be free of obstructions.

CHAPTER THIRTEEN
PEPÉ

Give thanks in all circumstances for this is
God's will for you in Jesus Christ.
—Thessalonians 5:18 NIV

Our ranch horses come from many different situations. Some are "surrenders" due to financial hardships the owners are facing. One was found loose on the highway, and after the state police got help rounding him up, he ended up at our place. Some were just donations for one reason or another. We've also received horses from other rescue organizations asking if we could take one or two.

When you see a horse after it's been abused or neglected, you can't comprehend why it happened. *Didn't anyone notice it was happening? Why didn't anyone do something?* However, when you witness it firsthand, it tests your true moral fiber and calls upon your courage.

Many children who visited our ranch were intimidated by the horses but enjoyed time with our two miniature horses. Unfortunately, most children were too heavy to ride the minis. At that time, our ranch had a variety of horses, but they were all average height. We felt that if God deemed it appropriate, we would add a pony to our herd. We prayed about it. The same week, we received an unexpected donation and put it away until we knew what to do with it.

Our daughter, Savanah, had just joined a 4-H horse group, and we were attending her first riding clinic. It was a two-day event with about twenty horses. I watched the clinician teach the children on horseback, and I noticed one particular little paint Arab. I've never been a fan of paint-colored horses, especially if their faces are all white. (They call such a horse a bald-faced horse.)

This pony was short but stout. What I loved most was his coloring—dark brown and white, but the brown was so dark that it looked black. His whole head was black, and his tail was black and white, like a skunk. This pony seemed to be the ideal size, so I asked the owner about him. I learned the pony was over thirteen hands high (that's about fifty-two inches at four inches per hand) and ten years old. He was low to the ground, solidly built, and had a short back so he could carry a little more weight. His conformation was good, and he was so affectionate. I thought, *This pony will be the standard for our pony search.*

Each stall housed a perfectly groomed and pampered horse, and Savanah loved them all. She walked through the stall area frequently over the two days and petted and talked to every horse. "Mom, look at this one!" "Mom, come here!" It gets a tad tiring when your child wants you to look at everything she finds amusing. Especially when she's such a horse nut and wants to collect them all.

After two days of that, Matthew and I went to rest in the truck, and I fell asleep. But I was awakened by my teary-eyed daughter. "Mom! You have to do something! That poor pony is being abused!" She told me she'd witnessed the owner of the pony enter the stall and attack him. She screamed at him while she pounded on him and kicked him.

Out of sheer desperation, the pony reared up to protect himself, and the owner backed out of the stall while screaming obscenities. "I can't wait to send you to the dog food factory!" was her last statement to the pony.

It was only then that she saw there were about a half-dozen witnesses. No one said a thing. The owner saw Savanah staring at her in shock. I think that because Savanah had frequently stopped at the pony's stall to pet him, the owner assumed Savanah might want him. In a very loud tone of voice, she asked Savanah, "Do *you* want him?"

"I'll go check with my mom" was Savanah's immediate response. She rushed to the truck and yanked the door open. "Mom, you have to save this pony before she kills him!"

I was still half-asleep, so I hadn't absorbed the whole story. I thought Savanah, a hormonal teenager, might have overreacted to the events. She went back to tending to her horse, and I went to talk to several of the witnesses. They all told me the same story.

At the end of the day, I prayed, and Matthew and I discussed buying the pony. We'd never encountered a situation like that. We didn't know what to do. We knew very little about that pony. Though I had witnessed two young girls riding him, we couldn't be sure he would be suitable for our program. Would he have too many unresolvable issues? We had many questions.

That's when Savanah said, "Mom, we were praying for a pony for the program. He's the perfect size and age, already trained, and if he has issues, we know enough people who know horses who can help work them out. If not, we can find him a good home."

So we said, "Okay. Let's go talk to the owner."

I tentatively approached the owner, unsure of the

best way to speak with her. I've said many times in this book how God has molded and shaped me for his purpose. I've been employed in customer service and sales all my life, and I know how to tolerate and talk to people no matter their personalities or moods. I knew from my experience that you can change the course of someone's intentions or mood with the right words.

After a brief greeting, we cut to the chase. She said, "He's up to date on all his shots, worming, and foot trimming."

Here goes nothing. "Would you take five hundred for him?"

She looked pensive. "I paid fifteen hundred for him, but he's no good to me, so if I can get five hundred for him, sure."

We learned later that she told many that she couldn't believe her luck to get $500 for a bad pony. Well, this "bad" pony let people he didn't know lead him onto a trailer with a horse he didn't know. He hesitated at the trailer door but then jumped on. He was visibly shaking, but it wasn't cold; he was scared but obedient.

We heard all kinds of comments from others as well as the owner about what a bad pony he was. That made me fearful, but I remembered to listen only to the voice of truth. That voice said this was the right thing to do no matter the outcome.

When we unloaded the pony, he was still shaking. But from that day forward, he was as good as gold. If he was a "bad" pony, I'll take a dozen please!

When Matthew noticed his tail was black and white, he said it looked like a skunk's tail. So we named him Pepé, after Pepé Le Peu. In case that's before your time, he's a charming cartoon skunk with a French accent.

Pepé quickly became a favorite at the ranch, and he was loving life. He was a totally different horse because he was secure in the knowledge that he wouldn't be beaten.

About ten months later, while he was being ridden, he began stumbling and running into things. Assuming he was just tired, we let him rest, but when his breathing became labored, we called the vet. The vet didn't have a diagnosis, but the blood test that she ran told her he was a very sick pony. The nearest emergency horse hospital was an hour and a half away. After a flurry of activity, we took off.

After some tests at the hospital, the second vet could find nothing. We agreed to keep him there overnight so they could run more tests in the morning. After a lot of testing, we still had no definite diagnosis, but an educated guess was that Pepé had a bacterial infection. We brought him home, but we had to go back a few days later when we saw he could barely stand.

Finally, after two lengthy says at the hospital, a battery of ultrasounds, X-rays, blood work and exploratory surgery, he showed slight signs of improvement and came home with strict orders for stall rest and medicine.

Five days later, I was running errands when Savanah called me from the barn. "Pepé's breathing really hard!" I told her that his fever had spiked the previous night but that he was getting antibiotics that seemed to help him that day. I said, "Just let him rest."

About every five minutes, I got a call from Savanah with an additional symptom. Pepé was going downhill fast. I called the vet. She said she'd be out immediately. I drove as fast as I could. My heart was racing. The fifteen-minute drive took an eternity. Driving became difficult. Tears filled my eyes. I was bawling.

The next call was barely audible. Savanah said between sobs, "Mom, he's lying down. He's shaking. I think he's dying! What should I do?"

When Pepé had come home the last time, I had a bad feeling he wouldn't make it, but I can't begin to express the sorrow in my heart for Savanah. You want to protect your children from pain and suffering, but sometimes you can't, and sometimes you shouldn't. To be a witness to death at such a young age is life altering. I didn't know what to say or tell her to do. I was hysterical myself. "Pray over him, baby, and love on him!"

My daughter sat alone with Pepé in his stall, shedding a river of tears and not knowing what to do for him. There was nothing she could do. She was experiencing the sorrow for Pepé that I was feeling for her. So she did what she knew. She comforted him. When he began to shiver, she covered him with blankets. When the life began to leave him, she stroked him and told him he was loved. She sang Matt Redman's "Bless the Lord" to him until his last breath.

Bless the Lord, oh my soul, oh my soul,
I worship his holy name. Sing like never before, oh my soul,
I'll worship your holy name …
Whatever may pass, whatever lies before me,
Let me be singing when the evening comes.
You're rich in love, and you're slow to anger
Your name is great, and your heart is kind.
For all your goodness, I will keep on singing

Ten thousand reasons for my heart to find …
And on that day when my strength is failing,
The end draws near and my time has come,
Still my soul will sing your praise unending
Ten thousand years and forever more!

I was still on my way when I got the last call, "Mom! Pepé's dead!" He had gone quickly. I thought she would be regretful that she had witnessed his death, but Savanah said that she was glad she had been with him and that he hadn't died alone. It was a time and a day she would normally have been at school. But as God would have it, there was no school that day, and she had been there to show compassion to a pony that had given us joy for ten months.

We give thanks to God for Pepé. We still don't know his exact cause of death, but we trust in God and his plan. We have a God who hears and answers prayers. Sometimes, the answer is no, and we can't see the good in that, but there's something to be learned, and in time, something positive will come from it.

The Lord gave and the Lord hath taken away;
blessed be the name of the Lord.
—Job 1:21 NIV

Pepé

CHAPTER FOURTEEN
FULL CIRCLE

But now finish doing it also, so that just as there
was the readiness to desire it, so there may be
also the completion of it by your ability.
—2 Corinthians 8:11 NASB

We received our first rescue horses in August 2011, and for almost four years, we fought our neighbors and the township authorities while caring for our horses in some of the most difficult conditions imaginable. We didn't feel it was wise to spend our finances drilling a well or installing electricity until we knew we could open the ranch.

In the meantime, we had to haul water in a water tank from the well at our home to the back of the property. On many occasions, due to the number of people living in our home (four children, foster children, and relatives living with us temporarily) and nine horses, the well ran dry, so we had to pay to have water delivered. We had to wear headlamps to see when we fed in the evenings in fall and winter as light was gone by 5:00.

Because we didn't have a barn, the horses stood in mud during the rainy months in spring and fall. It's a miracle we didn't have more than a handful of hoof and leg infections. The mud we walked through, at times, was so deep it sucked your boots off.

The weather didn't bother the horses at all, but without a building, we were exposed to the harsh elements. Many feedings took place in torrential downpours or in two feet of snow on top of thick ice. The grain wasn't so hard to carry, but the fifty-pound bales of hay were tough. Several winters were so intensely cold that the top four inches of our hundred-gallon water trough would freeze. We'd use a sledgehammer on the ice regularly and fish out the giant chunks to make sure the horses had drinkable water. But throwing out that ice meant we were wasting water and had to haul more over.

The weather made things difficult, and without stalls, feeding could be dangerous. When we entered the paddock, if we didn't attempt to control the situation, the horses would surround us and exhibit their dominance over each other. We could get caught in the middle of a tussle. So we put halters on each horse and tied each of them to an assigned tree where we mounted a feed bucket. Eventually the horses would go stand by their tree waiting to be hooked up. Then we would put the grain in their buckets.

On top of all that, local children came to our property and vandalized our paddock. They broke hay boxes we'd made to hold the square bales. They damaged the shelters, cut the fencing, and tied the horses' tails together. It was four years of learning. My friend affectionately called my four-year learning experience a trial by fire.

We finally received our 501(c)3 approval from the IRS in the fall of 2011. Hoping to appease our neighbors, we held a question-and-answer meeting to address their concerns. We kept to ourselves, so we thought we had a decent relationship with our neighbors. Some of our kids even played with theirs. However, at that meeting, we learned their true colors.

One neighbor said he didn't want a bunch of traffic on our dead-end road. In an attempt to compromise, we asked him if we could reduce the number of children visiting each day. We asked him how many cars per day would be acceptable to him. His response was "None."

Another neighbor was concerned that the children we were bringing to the ranch were juvenile delinquents who would break into their homes and rob them. Another said that having horses on our twenty acres would depreciate their home values. Ironically, our property couldn't be seen from the street because it was so densely wooded.

The most difficult thing to deal with was a verbal assault I took from a neighbor implying that I wasn't a good parent, so how was I going to help other children. I replied calmly (and with a poise that could have come only from God—because I was fuming inside) that she wasn't a perfect parent either; once, I had given her daughter a ride home from the bus stop because her grandmother had forgotten. She became enraged and screamed at the top of her lungs that I was crazy.

Before that meeting, I had prayed to God to give me the grace to handle the abuse that I was afraid I might get and keep me from bringing shame to His name. The fact that I didn't lash back at anyone is a testimony to the powers God can give you when you ask him. If I'd lost control like them, nothing else would have mattered; that would have been all they remembered.

In the spring of 2012, with the advice of an attorney, we acquiesced and applied for a permit. Part of the process of getting a permit was holding a public township meeting at which all township residents could voice their opinions. The same disgruntled neighbors, including Dan, repeated their objections. Dan had prepared a twenty-page document that listed every possible negative reason why we shouldn't be allowed to open our ranch—everything from how much manure a horse made every day to the annual number of horse-related injuries children sustained. What were we going to do with all that manure? Were we going to use a licensed manure hauler? *Really? A licensed manure hauler?*

Of course there was no mention of any positive effects. When asked what credentials we had that we could mentor children, my response was, "You don't need a degree to love a child." Dead silence. I smiled inside. So many of our friends and church family were there to support us. They spoke out for our cause; they said our community desperately needed a program like ours. Many defended our honor and asked all those who objected, "If you object so much, then tell me what *you* are doing for the kids of our community?" Again, silence.

When one neighbor said about us, "They don't care about anything but themselves!" one township supervisor became visibly irritated and raised his voice in protest on our behalf and said, "Selfish? How can they be selfish when they're trying to do this for others?" We knew that we had the support of at least one local government official.

In June, we received a permit with certain conditions that would cost us over $100,000 before we could open our doors. In addition, it would cost us $20,000 to hire an engineering firm to draw the designs to meet township requirements.

We spent the next twelve months raising money and finding an engineering firm. We hired a firm, and in August 2013, the plan was complete. We submitted it to the township planning commission. Even though our engineering firm had drafted plans to meet every requirement, we felt resistance at the very first meeting. It didn't help that the head of the planning commission was one of the neighbors on our street.

Our engineer attended the meeting and was disturbed at the amount of pushback we received. He heard some on the planning commission asking us to make changes that weren't required by their ordinances. Our engineer advised us to hire a lawyer, but that meant more money we didn't have. We were able to find an attorney who graciously volunteered his time, but it was to no avail. He couldn't find any resolution.

In December 2013, I became so discouraged that I just fell apart. We had been fighting the township for three years, and I was emotionally and physically exhausted. I was raising four children and having serious teenager problems, working two jobs, and taking care of nine horses. I battled depression regularly, but even with medication, I hit an all-time low.

I cried often that winter, but one instance sticks out. It was an exceptionally cold winter. Snow had begun to lay a white blanket on our beautiful woods. I was feeding the horses, and as I was breaking up the thick ice on top of the trough, my tears started. I smashed the ice with a hammer while sobbing out loud, "God, I can't do this anymore. You have to do it! I'm done!" I dropped the hammer, fell to my knees, and let the tears flow. Tenth Avenue North's song "Worn" became the theme song for that season of my life.

I'm tired, I'm worn, my heart is heavy from the
work it takes to keep on breathing.
I've made mistakes, I've let my hope fail.
My soul feels crushed by the weight of this world.
And I know that you can give me rest,
so I cried out with all that I have left …
Let me know the struggle ends, that you can
mend a heart that's frail and torn.
I wanna know a song can rise from the ashes of a
broken life and all that's dead inside can be reborn.
I know I need to lift my eyes up but I'm too weak,

life just won't let up.
I'm worn. My prayers are wearing thin.
I'm worn even before the day begins.
I'm worn. I've lost my will to fight.

Many of you have been there—so broken and so low that the only way is up. I had let my hope fail. I had taken my eyes off him. I was trying to do everything in my own strength. I was beaten, but God wouldn't let me quit. In 2 Corinthians 4:8–9 NIV, we read, "We are hard pressed on every side, but not crushed; perplexed, but not in despair; persecuted, but not abandoned; struck down, but not destroyed." I was right there.

In January 2014, God allowed Satan to use my children and our foster kids to add to my discouragement. They rebelled and made me ask myself, *If I can't raise my own children to make good decisions, what makes me think I can help other kids? Where did I go wrong? Am I fit to be a mentor?* In retrospect, I realize it wasn't the voice of truth but the deceiver's voice, and for a short time, I listened to it.

This battle continued well into late spring, but I held on; faith is believing in something you cannot see. I'd heard many sermons at church, but the one thing our Pastor Ed drilled into us that kept me afloat at that time was, "Faith is not a feeling, it's keeping your eyes focused on God no matter what the circumstances and no matter what you're feeling." So I continued to pray and believe and trust that God was in control and that if I held on, he would make things happen. And he did.

> *And let us not grow weary of doing good,*
> *for in due season we will reap, if we do not give up.*
> —Galatians 6:9 NIV

Mother's Day in 2014 was the turning point for our ranch. After a nice cookout, Matthew took our two sons to a driving range to hit some golf balls. On his way home, he decided to take a different route, a road he'd never been on. Then he saw it. A sign in a beautifully green, sprawling yard. "For Sale, 50+ acres Horse Farm with Barn."

Matthew called the number and spoke with the owner, Tom. After a long conversation, we asked if we could meet him to see the property. Tom was eighty-five; his wife had passed away just three months earlier. He was a friendly man but a stubborn wheeler-dealer. He owned much of the real estate in the area and rented it all—from storage units and office space to apartments.

We learned from others in the area that he had had the farm for sale for almost five years. Some folks we spoke to had viewed the property and had considered purchasing it, but they all agreed he wanted way too much based on the conditions of the buildings.

Being a real estate agent, I had a pretty good idea of its value, but Tom wanted what he wanted, and that was 50 percent more than what we thought it was worth. We negotiated for months but couldn't agree on a price. We suggested having an appraisal done, and in the end, he agreed to that.

Matthew and I struggled over purchasing the property. If it was what God wanted us to do, why was it so difficult? We took it as a sign that God was closing this door. After weighing the pros and cons, we backed out.

We went back to the township to see if we could work out the permit issues. Our attorney suggested having a meeting with all parties involved to make things easier. However, when I tried to arrange it, I got the runaround from the township manager. After a week of frustration, I threw up my arms and prayed for a sign as to what to do. It came immediately. *Duh!* God was telling us what to do, but we had lost our patience. In September, we asked Tom if he'd be willing to reconsider a sale to us, and he said yes. We had an appraisal done, which took three torturous weeks.

On October 7, prior to meeting with Tom, Matthew and I prayed, "Heavenly Father, we pray that this is your will. Lord, give us wisdom and the words to say." With a 107-page appraisal in hand, we met with Tom and went over facts and figures about the property and its location used to justify the appraiser's value. We offered Tom the appraised value.

Tom's response to the appraiser was, "He's full of sh**!" Even with all the hard facts, he didn't budge. My heart sank. When I told Tom, "No one's going to overpay for the property. It's just not good business," he said, "If they want it bad enough, they will."

We wanted it badly enough but just didn't have the money to meet Tom's price. *How can I appeal to him to change his mind?* When we asked God for the words to say before the meeting, I didn't believe he'd actually give them to me. It's amazing how much I limit him.

"Tom, how long has this property been for sale, four or five years? And in all that time, how many bona fide offers have you received?" I asked.

"Well, I've had lots of people looking."

"Yes, but were any of them serious buyers like us? We've been prequalified for a loan, and we have the down payment needed. You could wait longer for another buyer to come along, but why when you have ready and willing buyers right in front of you?"

And then a thought popped into my head—something I'd read in the appraisal that would increase the value of the property sale—mineral rights. I used the average value per acre and did the quick math in my head and gave him a final number.

"I'd consider that," he said.

Tom called me back eight days later to say he would accept our offer. I was dumbfounded. I dropped to my knees and thanked God for answering our prayers with a yes. The joy in my heart was indescribable. Ironically, the final amount was what we had originally offered him months earlier, the same amount he had refused. What changed his mind? Not facts and figures; he wasn't in a position where he had to sell. What changed his mind? We had prayed that God bring about a change in this stubborn man's heart and were shocked when he did it! Why? He's the almighty God!

> *Now unto him that is able to do exceeding*
> *abundantly above all that we ask or think,*
> *according to the power that worketh in us.*
> —Ephesians 3:20 KJV

I know unbelievers will say this was all coincidence, but consider these facts.

- We needed to be in the same township (it's only about thirty-three square miles) because we still had three children in school and didn't want to move them to a different school district.

- We needed to be close to Matthew's work (it's less than ten miles from this location).

- We needed it to be affordable.

- We needed it to have pasture, not a treed lot that would require a lot of money and work to clear for pasture. This property is a lot of pasture with a barn that has seventeen stalls *and* an indoor riding arena!

- The property had been for sale for almost five years, but the owner was not serious about selling or willing to come down in price. However, after his wife passed away, he knew he needed to downsize.

- I'm a real estate agent and couldn't find any other place suitable. This property was not listed in any resource I had access to; it was for sale by owner, so the only way to know about it was to drive by it.

The odds were stacked against us but Romans 8:31 NIV says, "What then, shall we say to these things? If God is for us, who can be against us?"

God is the great orchestrator of your life. If you believe in Him and seek him, he will open your eyes. He will show you the purpose for which you were created. He will prepare you for it. And I know from experience that you'll feel true joy for the first time in your life.

God's timing is impeccable. I felt that we suffered for five years, but looking back, I can see his perfect plan. I knew nothing about horses but learned so much in the past five years. He had stalled the ranch plans so I could learn how to ride and care for horses and figure out which ones would be good for our program. Five years to let my children grow up and move out or be more self-sufficient to allow me to put more time into the ranch. Five years for my youngest child to mature and gain wisdom to help manage our herd. Savanah does everything—scooping poop, feeding, first aid, vaccinating, worming, training, and exercising them. She met with the vet and farrier for their care. What a godsend! Five years of teaching me how to love my enemies (though I still struggle with that one).

For we are God's [own] handiwork (His workmanship),
recreated in Christ Jesus [born anew], that we may do those
good works which God predestined (planned beforehand) for
us [taking paths which He prepared ahead of time],
that we should walk in them [living the good life which
He prearranged and made ready for us to live].
—Ephesians 2:10 AMP

In the five years we waited, God allowed us to connect with people he wanted to be a part of our ranch. He provided for our needs and put us in touch with a circle of horse people who can help us with the ranch. He didn't allow us to build a barn; he used the township to stop us, thus saving the money for the new place he had in mind.

In those five years, he orchestrated the sale of my husband's family :business so I could be free to dedicate more time to the ranch. The odds of selling a bookbindery at a time when everything seemed to be going electronic didn't seem too good, but only a year after putting it up for sale, it sold!

Five years of God testing me to see if I would quit. To see if I was really committed to his purpose for me.

In this you rejoice, though now for a little while, if necessary, you have been grieved by various trials, so that the tested genuineness of your faith—more precious than gold that perishes though it is tested by fire—may be found to result in praise and glory and honor at the revelation of Jesus Christ.
—1 Peter 1:6–9 NIV

Five years of caring for horses outside in the harshest weather imaginable built my physical endurance. Five years of fighting perpetual resistance from the community and local government as well as battling family problems built my mental and emotional endurance but only because I stayed focused on God.

And not only that, but we also glory in tribulations, knowing that tribulation produces perseverance; and perseverance, character; and character, hope.
—Romans 5:3–4 NKJV

This ranch ... it's the song rising from the ashes of my broken life; without it, everything I had suffered would have been for nothing. I refuse to believe God would allow that for no reason. Only he can use a broken life for the good of others. I now want my life to be the proof of his love and existence.

Thank you for your interest in reading this book. If you enjoyed it or were touched and inspired by my testimonial, please consider making a donation to our ranch of hope and healing.

All proceeds from this book will go to:

Ready Yourselves Youth Ranch
115 Meehan Lane
New Brighton, PA 15066

WA